AT HOME IN GREECE

with 466 photographs

AT HOME IN GREECE

Julia Klimi

CONTENTS

CA2
NK
2051
A1
K58
2004

As the sun rises above the serene sea, the fisherman casts his nets into the Aegean – just as his ancestors have done over the ages – while making his way through the dangerous reefs concealed under the waves lapping at his boat. With a few deft flicks of his wrists, he gathers the nets up, now filled with silvery fish, almost blinded by the light.

Bathed in this wonderful light, contemporary Greek homes may be made of reinforced concrete, brick, iron and other modern building materials, but are based on ancient and yet eternal principles of colour, line, balance, moderation, harmony, simplicity and respect for nature. They are the natural extension of traditional architecture, infused with human values. Greek architecture, inextricably intertwined with Byzantium and Ancient Greece, continues to live on and is apparent in all works large and small. In essence, villages, towns and cities were not planned, but grew organically over the years out of the needs of the people. In this land of mariners, merchant sea captains, tradesmen and immigrants, the new is always accepted and absorbed, becoming in its own right an essential element of its inhabitants' expression. Here, all of the households illustrated are Greek in spirit, even if some of the owners are not Greek by birth.

Invaded time and time again by Romans, Venetians and Turks, and now by tourists – the Greek way of life has altered more in the last fifty years than in the previous thousand – over the centuries Greece has still managed to retain its own distinct style. It belongs neither to Europe nor to Asia and has been influenced by all that history has offered it through time. This mixture of elements from different cultures is represented in the book, with houses that bear the architectural features of Greece's eventful past: Ottomans in Rhodes, English settlers in Corfu, Venetians in Crete. The form and style of the settlements is the result of numerous factors: the inhabitants, the economy, the social structure, the traditions and customs, and geographical location, as well as the availability of building materials, the natural environment and the climate. These factors explain why settlements in close proximity are often so dissimilar in form and structure. It is this uniqueness that startles us today.

Each of the island groups and the mainland display rich variations of the Greek style, as can be seen in the pages that follow. The Cyclades, a cluster of islands with eternal houses, 'the archetypes of modern architecture' as Le Corbusier named them, stand out because of their simplicity. The villages sit on the rocks, so perfectly integrated with the landscape that they seem to be an extension of the sea and the mountains. The one-room cubic Cycladic house – dating back to Minoan settlements – is free of decorations and frills. Founded on the principle of economy and functionality, everything in the structure is designed a certain way for a reason. The flat roofs are slightly inclined to guide the rainwater to the cistern; walls are high to protect from the whipping winds; windows are small to block out the

INTRODUCTION

scorching sun; and walls are whitewashed to keep them clean, a need that became a custom and a symbol of joy and festivity.

The Dodecanese are scattered in the southeastern part of the Aegean and derive their name from the words *dodeca*, which means twelve, and *nese*, which means island. In the city of Rhodes, with palaces, arches, coats of arms and cobbled streets, one can imagine the sound of the hooves of horses belonging to the Knights of St John of Jerusalem who built the city. Lindos, stretching out next to the crystalline sea, boasts a little toy fortress at the peak of the hill surrounded by magnificent medieval walls. Imposing mansions, belonging to wealthy ship owners, tower over the narrow streets with flowering gardens and galleries. From the island of Symi, where neo-classical houses encircle the harbour, daring seamen set out to dive for sponges at the ends of the earth. Chora on the island of Patmos – charming, calm, mystical and carved by a labyrinth of white alleys – skirts the imposing Byzantine monastery. On the rest of the islands life goes on as it has for centuries, with a bustle in the ports where news and people come and go.

After four centuries of subordination to Venice and over two centuries to the Ottoman Empire, the towns of Crete possess a nostalgic air of an enchanting past. In Hania the Venetian influence is apparent in the tall houses, the harbour, which has a fortress, and the lighthouse. Unpainted for centuries, the houses have elaborate mouldings and stand proud in the winding alleys. Hidden arcades, fountains, galleries, Turkish mosques and minarets, and a bustling

marketplace are the pieces that make up the rich mosaic of the island's history. Rethymno, with its Venetian fortress, is similar. In contrast, the simple stone houses of the mountain villages seem to have been standing there since the Minoan Age. The large room in the centre of the house has a substantial fireplace, typical of the region, arched doorways and auxiliary rooms, while the courtyard is the centre of most activity. Apart from carrying out their daily chores here, this is where the hospitable Cretans welcome visitors with a glass of *raki* and a little something on which to nibble.

Among the Saronic Islands lie Hydra, with its beautiful little port, and Spetses, with its pinewood landscape. Both are romantic and once possessed a fabulous merchant marine. From the 18th century successful seafaring buccaneers and merchants built themselves opulent mansions, decorating them with various collections and pieces acquired on their travels to European cities. Today, the terraced gardens and pebbled patios offer a panoramic view of the picturesque harbours, free of cars.

With the rich ancient history of its legendary cities, such as Olympia, Sparta, Corinth and Mycenae, the Peloponnese are an amalgam of architectural styles. The Mani, dry and rugged, was cut off from the rest of Greece and its inhabitants learned to survive in adverse conditions. Its tall fortress houses and tower houses, fitted with many protective constructions, ensured security and storage for the bare essentials needed for survival. Today, travelling through the Mani one

is struck by the ochre stone of the houses, the Byzantine icons in the churches and the burning, vertical sunlight. At the southeastern tip is Monemvasia, a huge red rock tossed into the sea, crowned by a medieval town with a turbulent history. In the evening light it seems otherworldly as the walls are outlined against the sky and the silvery waves crash below.

A European wind blows through Corfu, the westernmost point of Greece. The old town of Corfu, elegant, cosmopolitan and refined, has a magical atmosphere and tall Venetian houses are reflected in the deep blue sea. A Western lifestyle and the high level of culture on the island have left their mark on the architecture. Surrounded by high walls and fortresses, the town features houses with many storeys, indicating the lack of space. Their interiors are a mixture of European styles that can only be called Corfiot. In the narrow streets, the lamp posts, the coats of arms and the relief walls tell the tale of the island's intriguing history. In the countryside, the aristocratic noblemen's villas still stand in dense forestation and vast, age-old olive groves. With an atmosphere of times past, the high-ceilinged rooms and the elegant furnishings are a successful combination of English and Venetian styles.

Scaling Mount Pindos through a dreamlike landscape, the houses of Epirus conceal within a rich décor of bright colours, in perfect contrast to the austere grey stone of their exteriors. The mansions, and also the smaller houses, the vaulted bridges, the fountains, the narrow streets and the public buildings found throughout mainland Greece are the masterpieces of the skilled craftsmen from Epirus. On Mount Pelion the top-storey extensions, the wood-carved ceilings, the embossed doors and the hand-painted walls all bear testimony to the region's prosperity.

Athens is home to the miraculous Parthenon and was the centre of the Golden Age dating back two and a half millennia. The capital of Greece – both ancient and modern – has always brought together all the elements of the Greek spirit. Alive and unpredictable today, it still reflects its glorious past.

Whether on the mainland or a far-flung island, a constant feature is the astonishing light in this part of the eastern Mediterranean. Greek light is an extraordinary phenomenon – coaxing the fish in the nets to glisten, painting the white Cycladic houses red at dawn, bouncing off Epirus stone with a metallic glint, blazing onto the whitewashed walls of the chapels at sunset, playing with the vaulted arcades of the houses in Patmos and Sifnos, reflecting on the blue and yellow stripes of the fishing boats. It is pure, natural, simple, dramatic and has always been a source of inspiration in every work of art created in this land. The philosophy of the Ionians, the Parthenon, the bare-breasted Minoan women of the Santorini frescoes, the glimpse of blue sea between two ancient columns, the dazzling white marble Cycladic idol: all these were born in this eternal light, linking past and present, bathing even the simplest objects in a sort of celestial, glow-worm hue. This incredible effect is revealed again and again in the photographs that follow.

From the arches of Sifnos and Amorgos, the dovecotes of sacred Tinos, the neo-classical manor houses of Syros, the picturesque, white villages of Paros, the rugged landscape of Serifos, the multi-coloured balconies of cosmopolitan Mykonos, the volcanic-rock *tholaria* of Astypalaia and Santorini, the variety of Cycladic architectural styles remains boundless. Fifty-six islands – some inhabited for over 3,500 years and some still uninhabited – are suspended in a sea of blue. The villages are usually located at the highest point of the island, a laby-rinth of narrow streets and tightly interwoven houses – the roof of one house serves as the patio of another. This is how the locals defended them-selves from invaders over the years. Ottomans, Venetians and Franks influenced the architectural style of each island, yet economic prosperity did not arrive until the 18th and 19th centuries. Here, life has always been harsh. The islanders lead a simple life – most of them used to live off the sea. In the mornings, after all-night fishing trips, the fishermen still dock in the harbours and exchange stories in the *kafenion* over an ouzo and meze.

The cascade of white houses, the blue dome of a chapel shining in the sunlight, the village square that suddenly appears round a bend, the chapel steps seemingly leading to God all create an architectural sculpture, illuminated and rounded, where no house is exactly like another, where there is no symmetry, no repetition. The ancient Greeks had a perfect grasp of the relationship between natural surroundings and man-made communities. In the Cyclades everything is created in moderation. The precise proportions between house and street – some alleyways are only wide enough for one person – give a natural sense of well being. There is an intuitive art in the creation of the spaces – art in the way each stone is placed in its proper place, illuminated just so by the sunlight, integrated with the landscape; there is art in the way the disorder of the sea is extended to the seeming disorder of the houses whittled by wind and wave.

With stone walls, small openings and smooth, curved surfaces, Cycladic houses are simple, cubic structures of either one or two storeys, their white exteriors dazzling the onlooker. Every feature is functional: from terraces and arcades to court-yards and balconies overlooking the sea; even the flat roofs are used to collect rainwater. Inside functionality is the key too: the main living area is organized to meet family needs. Stone, wood and cane are employed with a sense of economy and today the use of concrete is also widespread.

On most islands there are as many churches as days in the year. Monasteries are protected by high stone walls, family chapels are scattered over the bare and barren land studded only with prickly pear cacti and fig trees bent by the strong *meltemia* winds. Despite the boom of tourism over the last few decades, many things remain unchanged: the fishing with small colourful caïques, the cultivation of vineyards, the tiny, picturesque villages and the enjoyment of a miniature cup of strong Greek coffee in the shade of a pergola. Above all, Aegean light remains the essential element of architecture in the Cyclades, the womb of Mediterranean civilization.

THE CYCLADES

inhabitable sculpture

'We all have harmony within us', says Minas, a Greek designer who makes jewelry, *objets d'art*, furniture, houses – anything that conceals the primordial quality of life. His house on a winding Mykonian hill evokes the historical and mythical roots of the island. His lines are clean and his curves sensuous, reminiscent of the 5,000-year-old Cycladic civilization from which he derives his inspiration. It is a tradition that he carries on through his work, even with his own house-sculpture.

Virtually planted in the rock, well protected from the ruthless winds and merciless sun of the Aegean, the structure is northerly appointed – lending lucidity to both space and spirit – and elicits the harmony, grace, moderation and freedom of an ancient Greek statue. Far from the cosmopolitan bustle of Mykonos's sex, sun and clubbing lifestyle, this house-sculpture has been erected where there were once ruins, in the craggy landscape of rock and bush, and the rugged granite-chiselled beaches.

A succession of cubes with rounded corners follow a free-flowing curve of stone, plaster and lime, exuding the sense of having been there for centuries. In his organic forms there are no straight lines – only smooth surfaces and irregular, hand-chiselled spirals that define the walls, the steps and the niches with the blue of the sea peeking through. 'I find my inspiration in the purity of ancient Greece and the abstract forms of Cycladic art', says the artist. In this white house, ancient architecture and sculpture meet a contemporary outlook under the revealing light of the Aegean.

His materials – mud, stone, wood and marble – were used by the first inhabitants of the island. 'I had a dream', Minas says, 'that, with the exception of glass, I would make everything for the house myself. It was a challenge', he notes, 'to make my own doors, my own handles, my own locks with iron nails or screws.' Painted in the blue and white of the sea and sky, the house's doors, windows, locks, frames and even the screws are made of stainless steel, 'the only material that resists the ravages of the Mediterranean sea.'

The interior has only the basic necessities, common practice on Greek isles: a one-room house, almost spartan in style, divided into a sleeping area with an elevated bed with storage space, a small open-plan kitchen, a fireplace and a table. The one-room building is flanked by the bathroom and Minas's studio, once a stable. All the whitewashed buildings, situated around an enclosed courtyard, are linked by winding stairways that seem to roll between them, leading to a large, cool loft.

Minas moved to New York twenty-five years ago and established himself as a designer. In 1981 he returned to Athens and started to make jewelry in his own studio. His creations of silver, gold, steel, marble and porcelain are instilled with the perspective of the nameless yet wise Cycladic artisan. Whether it is a necklace, a cup, a clock or a bottle-opener, Minas always knows what to take away in order to create his simple, energy-filled forms inspired by nature.

OPPOSITE In the dry and barren Mykonian hills the white cubic house of Greek sculptor Minas blends in perfectly with the Cycladic landscape.

ABOVE Located at the highest point of the grounds and of the whole island, the sun dial catches the complete course of the sun. The gold dial indicates the time, while the seasons are engraved on the Penteli marble.

LEFT Overlooking Ftelias Bay, a stone wall hems in the ten-acre estate, freely following the lie of the land.

OVERLEAF The sculpted form of the house on the rock and the whitewashed stucco that enfolds the gently rounded structures represent building techniques that date back 5,000 years to when the Cycladic civilization flourished here.

OPPOSITE, ABOVE, LEFT A quiet niche of cane-roofed sheds sheltered from the winds is the ideal hideaway on a hot afternoon.

OPPOSITE, ABOVE, RIGHT In the style of the local architecture, the gently rounded forms, each catering to specific needs, provide protection from the winds.

OPPOSITE, BELOW, LEFT Bougainvillaea, fig and date trees, along with herbal shrubs, surround the old well in the garden.

OPPOSITE, BELOW, RIGHT A brow over the windows protects them from rainwater, while the groove around the house safeguards against damp.

ABOVE, LEFT The courtyard table is formed from a marble lip protruding from the wall.

ABOVE, RIGHT The kitchen adheres to a minimalist philosophy. A graceful sterling silver candleholder by Minas rests on the African walnut counter.

BELOW, LEFT The earthy tones of the bathroom and the walls, limewashed to allow them to breathe, create a sympathetic backdrop to the interplay of sculptural forms.

BELOW, RIGHT A bean-shaped table made of American beech echoes the shape of the studio.

the house around the rock

One of the most emblematic domestic architectural works to have been built in recent years on the Greek isles is Akis and Molly Tsiringaki's house on Mykonos, which is bright white, cube shaped and perfectly proportioned. The ensemble majestically stretches in its desert-like site suspended over the Aegean Sea, with a breathtaking swimming pool that extends into the house. On the highest point of the hill above the town, it battles with the strong northerly winds, known as the Aegean *meltemia*, and recalls the simplicity of line in the local villages.

Commissioned as a holiday home for the Athenian family, the project was entrusted to Barcelona-based architect Javier Barba and the Greek interior designer Kirios Criton. When the architect arrived to survey the site he was confronted with a large jutting rock and a salamander sunning itself on its surface. That was the moment when the idea of building the house around the rock was born. When the interior designer created the décor he employed the salamander as his theme.

Using spiralling lines and sensual surfaces, Barba wished to express himself in the language of the land – before designing the house, he visited numerous monasteries, churches, windmills and mountain villages, where whitewashed houses tumble down the mountainsides and labyrinthine streets meander through. The exterior walls are awash with the white lime that reflects the light and keeps the interior cool. A dome similar to those seen on monasteries sprouts from the flat roof. Inside, the corridor linking the bedrooms can be likened to the narrow streets of Mykonos, with its successive doors and a glass roof diffusing the sunlight.

OPPOSITE The pure Cycladic lines of the white structures float alongside the linear walls made of local stone, while the swimming pool brings them together as it flows right into the house.
RIGHT Chestnut beams span the hand-shaped walls, whitewashed according to the age-old practice, as is the dome that the architect 'borrowed' from a Mykonian monastery.

Barba very much wanted to use the age-old, thoroughly Cycladic methods and materials without sacrificing a modern approach. Lined up in a row, but each of different length, which allows for more light, every room sports French doors instead of the small and numerous windows found in traditional houses. They all open out from the ground floor onto the garden, as Barba wanted the interior and exterior to co-exist in harmony. 'Architecture cannot surpass Nature', he says. A pebbled mosaic floor depicting a salamander leads to the enclosed garden. In the background the rock is half inside and half outside the house, seemingly sliced by a glass plate. In this way, even from the outside, the gaze can glide unhindered through the house to the waters of the pool and sea beyond.

Working on the interior, Kirios Criton used the traditional techniques of the Mediterranean. The walls are tempered white, recalling the dampness of old homes. The ceilings are grooved by chestnut beams – as in all Mykonian houses – which are painted white like the oakwood floors. In the kitchen there is a chiselled marble skirting board from the neighbouring island of Tinos. The true works of art, however, are the basins in the bathrooms which are crafted from the same marble. The sole modern material is the stainless steel used for the kitchen fittings.

The furnishings have been selected for their simple lines and the natural colours of the fabrics tie in with the neutral tones of the walls. There are few decorative objects, designed by Christian Liaigre and

Andrea Branzi, while only the 19th-century wood carved doors have been reclaimed from old houses.

Around the rock core of the house, the living spaces spread out freely, allowing the natural light to flood into them. The architect has left the greenhouse, the living room and the adjoining dining room to roll into one another on two levels, separating them by a low wall that also functions as a counter.

The swimming pool area has wooden sun decks protected from the raging *meltemia* and the crashing waves by ingeniously placed stone walls designed by Kirios Criton, enclosing the large living and dining room. With the barriers of interior and exterior falling away, the owners can sun themselves next to the pool and take a siesta in the shade, just like any inhabitant of the Cyclades.

OPPOSITE The sculpted niches, the oak floors, the modern furniture made of natural materials and the off-white colour give a uniformity to the sitting room that has embraced the rock at the core of the house.

BELOW, LEFT The motif in the pebblestone represents the salamanders that sun themselves in the courtyard.

RIGHT A stone wall protects the terrace dining area from the strong northerly winds. The table with a mosaic depicting a tree was designed by Kirios Criton; the chairs are by Philippe Starck.

BELOW, RIGHT Half inside and half outside the house, the rock was incorporated in the structure that draws energy from it. The front door and the kitchen doors were discovered in an antique shop.

ABOVE Part of the bathroom wall, inspired by a Mykonian house where earthenware jugs were stored in the niches, holds a tree sculpted by Andrea Branzi. The chair is made of driftwood.

RIGHT Two chiselled marble basins, the work of an artisan from Tinos, are positioned on a concrete counter. The storage space below is covered with rattan.

ABOVE The bedroom has an air of
tranquillity due to the off-white colour
scheme that uniformly diffuses the light.
The room is furnished with a Christian
Liaigre wood and iron bed and an Apta
armchair by B&B Italia.

living on the beach

Tinos is a barren and rugged island, relentlessly whipped by the northern winds that shape the rocks like a sculptor does his block of stone. On this unspoilt Cycladic island, where the dovecotes sprout like natural sculptures, there is a centuries long tradition of marble sculpting. Many world famous Greek sculptors were born here. The landscape is dotted with stone villages and a dirt road leads to the grandiose bay of Kalivia – the name refers to the many 'huts' that used to be there. A few still remain today.

It is not that many years since Virginia Ventouraki, a representative of one of the largest European Furniture and Design firms in Greece, and her husband Seraphim Fyntanidis, editor-in-chief of a leading Athenian newspaper, chose Tinos as the site for their retreat. Commissioned as a holiday home, the project was entrusted to the Athenian architect Zeppos-Georgiades & Associates. Their prestigious track record includes successful combinations of modern and traditional Greek architecture.

The dominant feature is the stone wall which tapers into the swimming pool. The house is built on various levels, following the natural lay of the land, while all exterior and interior spaces open out onto the sea. At first glance the construction may seem to have more in common with a Mediterranean aesthetic, but on closer inspection the very real influence Cycladian style has had on the architectural conception becomes apparent. The stone used for the walls of the house, for example, is from the local quarry. On one side the house takes the shape of an old hut and is made of the same stone as the rocks surrounding it. Local marble flagstones have also been extensively used for the terrace and all the exterior spaces. The building's form, particularly

the austere exterior, evokes the flat-roofed cubic houses of the island. The positioning of the rectangular courtyard at the centre of the house to protect it from the summer *meltemia* is a practice that dates back to Minoan times.

The sculpted curved surfaces in the interior create small niches, rounded staircases and *sofas* (built-in beds), while the ceilings sport the traditional thick, untreated wood beams.

The owners often entertain so they wanted to make the kitchen the nucleus of the house. Other spaces evolve from the kitchen and have large openings that ensure a direct view of the landscape and the seascape, uniting the interior with the exterior. From the large veranda one can look out over the sea as it changes from deep blue to sky blue, white and turquoise, and sniff the northern breeze carrying along with it all the scents of the grounds: thyme, rosemary, lavender and lemon blossom.

The furnishings are simple and modern, designed in the spirit of comfortable holiday living, including

pieces by famous designers and manufacturers, such as Kartell, Cassina, Vico Magistretti and Piero Lissoni. Works of art by Greek and other European artists provide cheerful contrasts, complementing the contemporary feel of the interior. The colours are those of the Cyclades: indigo blue, ochre and pine green, but echoed in lighter shades: ochre has become lemon yellow, pine green is pistachio nut green, while the indigo remains the same. The white-painted, pitch-pine floors take on an intensive blue tone at sunrise fading to orange at sunset. The colours set a happy tone for the house.

Designed using a free interpretation of Cycladic architecture, the house is thoroughly anchored in its site and simple and intelligent in its conception. An example of this is the swimming pool, which is original in design and grand in scale. It is flush against the exterior stone wall, while the steps on the veranda keep going right into the pool. As for the owners and their guests, they live in and out of the water, trailing sand and having siestas in the shade, while a white fishing boat appears from behind the rock and seems to wave to the dovecote up on the hill.

PRECEDING PAGES, LEFT The stone wall disappearing into the pool is on the same level as the sea and the beach.
PRECEDING PAGES, RIGHT The stone exterior harmoniously blends with the landscape.
OPPOSITE, LEFT A bath sculpted out of coloured concrete.
OPPOSITE, RIGHT Cycladic architecture with a modern twist: a ceiling of rough hewn wooden beams, a wide pitch-pine floor and a Tom Dixon wicker chair.
ABOVE The white ceiling and floor accentuate the brightly coloured walls. The fireplace was designed by the architects, the couches are by Cassina Met and the leather Frog chairs are Piero Lissoni for Living.

ABOVE Curved niches in the wall form the bookcase. The island-style *sofa* happily coexists with the Cappellini armchair and the handmade curtains.

ABOVE, LEFT The traditional indigo blue of
the Cyclades brightens up the bedroom
with a simple fireplace designed by Eleni
Georgiades.

ABOVE, RIGHT Indigo walls set off the white
Italian Cyrous bedroom set.

perched on a volcanic rock

A reddish black rock in the southern Cyclades is all that is left of Santorini – 3,500 years ago half the island sunk into the abyss following a tremendous volcanic eruption – making it one of the world's most fascinating islands. The whitewashed village of Oia has achieved its own greatness: first as a farming village and now as a holiday destination and 'douceur de vivre'. A dramatic site, looking across the caldera, with the sea fading into the sky and a rugged landscape, it offers little protection from the burning sun and the tricks of the Cycladian winds. Troglodytically niched into the volcanic rock, the traditional homes of the dazzling, whitewashed village cling to the brink of the caldera.

At the topmost point of the village, where sky meets land and black rocks of the caldera touch the vast blue of the Aegean, sits a domed, stone house – perched like a gull's nest. Stark white on

the black volcanic rock, it stands in perfect harmony with the Santorini landscape.

It was only natural for Kostas Psychas, a Santorini devotee since he visited the island with his parents as a child and now owner of one of the most attractive hotels, to create a house that respected the architecture of the island. He was so inspired by the environment that he decided to design the house himself and help with its construction.

The large, high domes are clearly sculpted and the whole is a successful rendering of the Santorini home in a totally contemporary way. Due to the singularity of the ground – soft volcanic dirt – domed houses built in the earth have always been widespread on the island. Employing local redstone and modern-day concrete for the domes, the

building does not have any corners whatsoever. This is because traditional modes of construction were followed, so the craftsmen could not carve corners out of the stone and created curves and arches instead. The house, with its softened lines, is exquisitely simple in form. Built on one level in an open-ended square form, the courtyard lies at the centre, where all the activities of the home take place. Opposite the open end is the domed living area and on the other two sides are the bedrooms. All of the spaces lead to one another via small or large openings and arched doorways, while retaining their autonomy. Every aspect of the house is unique – there is no repetition, no symmetry. The windows are sometimes large and sometimes shrink to portholes and then widen again to skylights.

The sunrays bounce off the surfaces during the course of the day and lend different perspectives to the white, austere interior. It is a bright setting. Basic form and material are explored – humble objects such as sea pebbles provoke a new look at everyday island living. Ideas and forms are reawakened by a touch of sculpture, such as in the fireplaces, the oven and the chimneys, which the owner created with the help of an old craftsman.

The courtyard opens out onto the tip of the peninsula with a view of the craggy rocks of the caldera on one side and the fertile valley on the other. All around the vast blue sea dominates the landscape. Awash with grand Cycladic light and a permanent light breeze, this house is a sailboat floating on the Aegean.

PRECEDING PAGES, FAR LEFT The vast blue sea stretches beyond the low garden wall; MIDDLE The style of the dwelling is reminiscent of the island's old houses; RIGHT The path leading to the house is made of black sand from the beach mixed with cement.
BELOW Local limestone frames all the openings, including the front door; RIGHT The tradition of rounded corners dates from when the workers had no way of cutting the volcanic black and red stone.
OVERLEAF, LEFT The curved forms lend charm to the bedroom; RIGHT Utter simplicity in the domed sitting room where natural materials, including marble from Naxos and firwood for the floors, reign.

the house of art

Like a pebble tossed in Odysseus's path, halfway between Troy and Crete, the Cycladic island of Paros has always been celebrated for its snow-white marble. Coveted by sculptors over the ages, it was used for the renowned Venus de Milo and the Winged Victory of Samothrace, which are both in the Louvre in Paris. With this natural resource, the tiny windswept island has no need for tourism like its neighbours. Here life goes on at an easy pace – with the cleaning of nets of minuscule fish, the pounding of octopus on the rocks and the sipping of ouzo in the port taverns.

Lefkes is a peaceful mountain village where the architectural style has been left unspoilt. Adorned by the colourful façades of neo-classical houses and with winding narrow streets, the village enjoyed great prosperity in the 19th century due to the marble quarries and its status as the island capital.

When the young Athenian Maria Demetriades first visited the village she was immediately smitten by the old oil press building standing in the middle of a vineyard. Having adopted the island as her own, today she spends a large part of her time there, while also running Medusa, an art gallery in Athens, where some of the best-known Greek artists exhibit their work.

Naturally, the house she has created is a living work of art. The harsh, rugged industrial form appealed to her, and so the stone on the thick walls is exposed, while inside there are no dividing walls, heightening the sense of expansiveness and freedom she prefers. With its vast spaces, it is a perfect holiday home and particularly comfortable because of the spacious common areas and the rooms around them with their marble-flagged floors. The old local marble has also been extensively used for the terrace and the large bathroom – the olives were originally rinsed here – where the old vat now functions as a bath. The basin is a piece of art, designed by Maria herself. Stone and wood are today, as they were then, the favoured decorative materials. The impact of the structure is subtle, starting from the six-metre (20-ft) high traditional ceilings with its old chestnut beams and the intervening cane down to the white walls reflecting the Aegean sunlight.

The bright, natural light streaming in through the large wood frame windows and doors enhances the works of art scattered throughout the space. Some of the most significant contemporary Greek artists are represented here: Nakis Tatsioglou, Giorgos Rorris, Yorgos Gyparakis, Panos Raymondos and Yiannis Demetrakis. The sparse furnishings, unique pieces by Greek designers, such as the world-renowned Takis, as well as other samples from large design firms such as Arflex and Philippe Starck, simply complement the minimalist yet artful stage.

The garden puzzle-paths of Parian marble lead to the vegetable garden with its ripe red tomatoes, a delight to pick and rinse off in the spring water. In the evening, Maria and her guests gather on the terrace overlooking the white roofs of the village glowing among the olive trees. Her candle-lit get togethers in the sunset are a magical affair. The magic is enhanced by Takis's *Signals* which commune with the universe just like the house and garden, which have waited there from times past to become the most natural and clear expression of Maria's dream.

OPPOSITE, LEFT The Parian olive press
building was converted into a comfortable
home which retained much of its old
functional appearance inside and out. Here,
kittens are frolicking in the courtyard with
Anita Argyroiliopoulou's sculpted lizard.
OPPOSITE, RIGHT Maria Vlandi's Cycladic idol
nestles among the grapevines.
RIGHT An old stone wall frames the kitchen
where Takis's table steals the show; the
chairs were designed by Verner Panton.
The room is heated by the wall oven.

BELOW The modern B&B Italia leather bed
contrasts with the mural depicting human
figures that Yiannis Demetrakis painted
on the wall of the old cistern.

ABOVE, LEFT With an industrial atmosphere, the living room coordinates with the Arflex couches and the metal table designed by Maria Demetriades. The two lights were designed by Takis and the sculpture next to the fireplace belongs to the sculptor Panos Raymondos.
ABOVE, RIGHT The olives were once rinsed in the Parian marble bathroom. Maria Demetriades designed the counter with the basins; the tree and bee sculptures were made by Anita Argyroiliopoulou.

cycladic modern

Surrounded by water, but always parched, the Cycladic island of Paros features many of the elements considered quintessentially Cycladic. Lio Aurelio was enchanted by the barren, rolling landscape with hills tapering to the sea, the vast golden grain plains with wheat waving when caressed by the wind and the scattered white cube-shaped houses. The well-known Swiss architect, along with his wife Lola-Lorenza Galfetti, has been travelling around the Cyclades for the past thirty years, drawing inspiration for his work from the authentic island architecture and the relationship of the structured environment with the sky, sea, earth and man.

Aurelio's dream to build a modern holiday home in an unspoilt environment on the south-westernmost point of the island recently came true. Guided by the essential element of Aegean light and the lay of the land, he created smooth surfaces with

a unique harmony and plasticity that perfectly tie in with the landscape. From a simple architectural project – two identical, parallel buildings, featuring a large courtyard with palm trees in the middle – a form was born with free-flowing comfortable spaces and clean lines that stretch towards the vastness of the sea, allowing the gaze to wander from north to south. In an advantageous location on a hill, his new refuge, rectangular in shape, is made of the red stones of the surroundings. One of the block structures comprises the main house and the other the guesthouse.

The original and inventive design consists of a series of linear walls. The exterior wall, interrupted by doors leading to the courtyard, is dressed in stone to unify the complex with the landscape. The interior is like a long, wide corridor punctuated by patios shaded by white awnings, which are lowered when the need arises. Sliding doors serve to divide

BELOW The house consists of a long gallery with linear smooth surfaces. A second gallery is used as a guesthouse – it hides behind the exterior wall made of stone, tying the house perfectly to the landscape.
OPPOSITE, ABOVE The courtyard, strewn with white marble gravel, is for the architect an empty space that links the sea with the mountain. Aluminium doors interrupt the linear quality of the wall.
OPPOSITE, BELOW The large terrace seems suspended over the flawless Cycladic landscape.

ABOVE **Two Ron Arad chairs designed for Moroso**
are perfect for gazing out from the veranda onto
the barren Cycladic landscape of the hills of
Paros and Antiparos and the sea.

OPPOSITE, ABOVE **Playful shadows created by**
the Cycladic light: this essential element guided
Aurelio to create smooth surfaces of unique
harmony and plasticity.

OPPOSITE, BELOW **A succession of spaces,**
alternately covered and open, allows the dwellers
to enjoy the breeze, the mountain and the sea.

the space and become transparent walls. Nothing interrupts the clean lines of the surfaces: everything is hidden behind plaster panels, which do not touch the ceiling, concealing cupboards, bathrooms and storage rooms. The white walls unify the total space and the people living within provide the colour. The series of alternately open and closed 'rooms' – the sitting room, kitchen, dining room and bedroom – culminate in the veranda. This unique gallery overlooking the sea is open to the air, the light and the sea brine, lending an incredible sense of freedom to the inhabitants.

Functionality is the real key to the project – even the materials employed are basic. The floors, both inside and out, are made of reinforced concrete. Stone was used for the exterior walls, painted cement for the kitchen, and metal and glass for the sliding doors. The modern and minimalist furnishings play with materials and colour. Everything is light and fluid in the spirit of the holiday makers' nomadic lifestyle. The décor is minimal with only abstract forms. Made of plastic or aluminium, mostly designed by Kartell, Ron Arad and Martin Van Severen with some by Aurelio himself, the decorative pieces are bright splashes of colour in the all-white spaces.

The architect's concept is a free reinterpretation of Cycladic style from a modern viewpoint, where the courtyard was the centre around which all the activities of the home revolved. Simplicity of form and frugality have always allowed the landscape to show through. The relation of nature to the building is all pervasive: there is not a single spot where you cannot see it, feel it or hear it. The view of the sea, the morning breeze, the coolness of the night and the sparkling stars even permeate the bedrooms.

The magical and limitless Cycladic sunlight paints the white rooms a different shade each hour of the day: blue at dawn, red at dusk. The sunset is always a spectacle not to be missed. From the large veranda you can watch the sun dive into the fiery sea right next to the island of Antiparos as the palm trees gently rustle in the breeze.

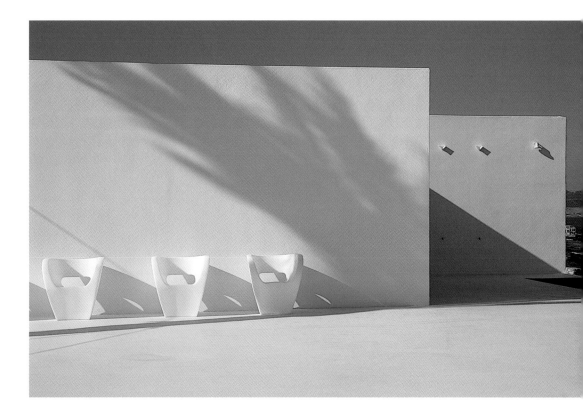

ABOVE Just for fun, Aurelio placed the bath
behind the bed, sinking it into the cement floor.
The chests of drawers were designed by Antonio
Citterio for Kartell and the chair is a Philippe
Starck piece.

OPPOSITE, ABOVE The Martin van Severen chairs
for Kartell give a splash of colour in the all-white
sitting room.

OPPOSITE, BELOW In the kitchen the refrigerator
and the shelves are positioned behind an interior
wall that does not meet the ceiling. The tables
were designed by Aurelio and the chairs by Ron
Arad for Kartell.

a stage hewn in stone

As visitors approach the Serifos port of Livadi by boat they are blinded by the whiteness of cube-like houses scaling the hill to the very top. The houses are punctuated by windmills whose sails used to turn night and day when working in the iron mines was the main occupation of the inhabitants. When the mines suddenly closed in the early 1960s there was a mass exodus of young people from the island and the stone houses gradually deteriorated due to the onslaught of the strong Aegean winds.

Now there are only traces of the roofs that were thatched with seaweed and cane and covered in clay. But fortunately a few people seeking the serenity

BELOW As though a sculpture, the rock has been incorporated into the décor along with the flagstones and the cane ceiling.
RIGHT Spaces hewn from the rock create the setting for a summer siesta. The staircase, the fireplace and the built-in couch with a traditional cotton mattress all cater to simple comforts. The wooden details were painted grey as was the custom before the modern trend of painting them blue.

and beauty of island life disembarked here, filled with passion and love for the place. Helped by the elderly inhabitants who still remembered the techniques of the old artisans, these people took on the task of rebuilding the small houses – the white wreath laid on the crown of the hill.

Manolis Pandelidakis was one of the first of these new 'settlers'. Today, the well-known set designer divides his time between his Athens home and his house in Chora, the main town of Serifos, which has a beautiful vista of the rocky landscape and the sea. He and his friend Yiorgos Zafeiriou, a civil engineer, created new spaces and remodelled several old houses – in the past a house consisted of just one room – into a single home. Built on four levels, on the edge of a precipitous cliff, the house is adapted to the shape of the rock, seemingly sprouting from it. The whole island of Serifos is a rock, so Zafeiriou wanted it to be the dominant element of the house, revealing its presence in every room.

With some rooms small and some large, most of them hewn out of the rock, left untreated as part of the walls, the house is reminiscent of a cave dwelling. Only local materials, some reclaimed – large stones from nearby ruins, kitchen counters, stone basins, old doors and tiles – and techniques were used. The local builders made everything by hand and the interventions are not obvious as it all seems so natural: the chiselled interior staircase, the chimney, the built-in couches and the beds.

BELOW The Cycladic simplicity of a chapel, a terrace, the sea, the sky and the Aegean light. OPPOSITE Two old churches – Christos and Agia Varvara – serve as a playground for the sunrays. One's gaze is dazzled by the whitewashed buildings and turns to the blue sea.

The Cycladic style and the very real influence of
the surroundings are all too apparent in the house –
in the wooden door and window frames, which have
been painted grey, as was the habit in times past,
rather than the blue used in more recent years;
in the nooks and crannies in the stone walls; and
in the flagstones accentuated by the lime grouting.
The restricted range and 'poverty' of the materials
employed is true to the Cycladic tradition whereby
the few elements that are at hand are used in an
economical, but distinctive, manner. The roofs
were redone with beams and cane, and only the

outer layer of clay was replaced with cement,
transforming the roof into a solid terrace that
did not exist previously.

The furnishings are simple and innovative with
some recycled pieces and others bought from
antique shops, easily complementing the island
style. Other age-old Cycladic devices are also
employed: the impression of coolness and stillness
that greets the visitor when entering the house;
the use of white throughout the interior as a reprieve
from the brightness outside; the openings that
have been strategically positioned to maximize

air circulation. The final touch to the set was
given by Pandelidakis's own hand. He masterfully
matched motifs and colours, tempered the
wooden floors, painted the kitchen tiles, refinished
all the furniture in the tones he desired, and
hung model ships he crafted himself from the
ceilings and on the walls. And so he created his
own personal space: the retreat of an artist who
often seeks refuge here to work in peace in
a monastic atmosphere while looking out at the
vast blue sea – an effect that could be nothing
but dramatic.

BELOW On the third storey, the studio is a place where the artist can find inspiration.
ABOVE, RIGHT An old platter and jug from the set designer's collection sit in a marble sink.
RIGHT, MIDDLE Pandelidakis masterfully painted the kitchen tiles.
BELOW, RIGHT The original features were left intact in the entrance.
OPPOSITE, ABOVE A stage set with the artist's favourite model boats as its theme.
OPPOSITE, BELOW, LEFT A traditional bed and old mirror in the bedroom.
OPPOSITE, BELOW, RIGHT The whitewashed surfaces play hide and seek with the sun in the bathroom.

classic cycladic scene

As the wind whistles through the whitewashed alleys of Chora on Serifos it whips into the village square with its neo-classical houses and small café on the corner. The maze of streets and terraces connected by whitewashed staircases and courtyards is woven together so naturally that one is surprised that the planning is incidental, growing out of the incline of the ground, the weather conditions and the local inhabitants' needs.

All the roads lead to the medieval fortress and directly below it, on a steep cliff, is the white house with the blue-green shutters that belongs to Yiorgos Zafeiriou. Enamoured by the Cyclades for decades, he discovered the island many years ago and loved it

at once, the almost primitive simplicity suiting him perfectly. Since then he has spent his summers here.

From the garden gate you can see the port of Levadi and the neighbouring vegetable gardens. In the background lies the expanse of blue sea, with the fishing boats coming and going. The stone house with its blue-green shutters, the narrow passageways, the whitewashed walls and the balconies suspended over the landscape are the epitome of Cycladic style. The impetus for the blue and white look that dominates the interior came from the whiteness of the surroundings and the blueness of the sea and the sky; the whole structure plays with the contrast between inside and out.

BELOW, LEFT The shapes, scale and colours of the local architecture are echoed in Zafeiriou's white house with blue-green shutters, an idyllic holiday retreat.
BELOW, RIGHT The vista from the balcony of Chora's white houses and the mountain is unique.
OPPOSITE Perched on the precipitous rock at the highest point of the main town of Chora on Serifos, the white house seems suspended between the sky and the land.

The cubic impact of the house is softened by the surroundings. The small roof terraces on different levels were redesigned to meet the dwellers' needs at various times of the day. As a civil engineer, Zafeiriou was inspired by the local architecture to design a traditional two-storey house adapted to modern needs and situated directly in the living rock. The two smaller buildings, the guestrooms, reflect the older practice of having an out house and an outside oven.

Light is an essential element of the house and so the openings have been designed to take advantage of it. Some of the windows are small, some are french doors, while other doors are split like stable doors – in the past these doors served to keep the domestic animals out, while today they allow the house to be properly aired. A few of the rooms have been carved out of the rock, such as the dining room and the small guesthouse in the garden, where the rock was left untreated to remind the house dwellers of the house's origins. Zafeiriou kept to natural materials, which chimed with his simple lifestyle on the island. He played with shapes, curves, spaces, colour and light in order to discover the primordial essence of things. He designed the furniture himself and chiselled the decorative objects out of pieces of marble found on site. Inspired by nostalgia and employing imagination, they teach a lesson in simplicity. Nothing is superfluous. What else does a timeless place like this need if not a built-in Greek-style bed, a mosquito net, a few sea urchin shells and a kitchen filled with old pots and pans, baskets and red enamel crockery?

The vast Aegean sea, calm at some times and choppy at others, continues to call up the local myth of Perseus, who, according to legend, was washed ashore on Serifos in a wooden crate after his mother Danae put him out to sea to save him from his grandfather's rage. When he reached manhood, he rescued the inhabitants by slaying Medusa, the wicked mermaid. Thus the timeless Aegean feeds the island with myths of heroes and mermaids and all these elements are called into play in Zafeiriou's Cycladic retreat.

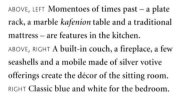

ABOVE, LEFT Momentoes of times past – a plate rack, a marble *kafenion* table and a traditional mattress – are features in the kitchen.

ABOVE, RIGHT A built-in couch, a fireplace, a few seashells and a mobile made of silver votive offerings create the décor of the sitting room.

RIGHT Classic blue and white for the bedroom.

ABOVE The white room is bathed in Cycladic light.
Authenticity and simplicity are revered here.

The medieval city of Rhodes, the neo-classical serenity of Symi, the Byzantine settlement of Patmos, the volcanic landscape of Nisyros, the traditional houses of Karpathos, the Venetian castle in Astypalaia, the sophisticated manor houses of Kastelorizo and Halki, this cluster of rocky islets and atolls called the Dodecanese numbers more than twenty. The singularities of the landscape and the varying histories determined the form of the architecture. The glory of Byzantium, the influence of the Venetians and Franks, the proximity to the Greek cities of Asia Minor, Ottoman – and later Italian – rule which they managed to throw off in 1912, only to be placed under Italian rule until they were able to cede to Greece in 1948, and the emigration of their inhabitants to the four corners of the earth are only a small part of the history of the Dodecanese. The islands came back into the limelight with the boom of tourism, delighting everyone near and far with the blue sea and crystalline air.

From the 17th century the wealth of the world-travelled sea captains and ship owners of Lindos was reflected in their residences. Domes with daring openings, lining arches, Gothic themes, wood-carved and hand-painted ceilings, court-yards laid with pebblestones, skylights of stained glass and incredible murals can all be found.

Patmos, the island where St John wrote the Apocalypse in AD 95, is a dreamlike land where it is easy to forget apocalyptic foretellings. The peaceful town of Chora, brimming with religious mysticism, is crowned by the fortress-like monastery of St John Theologos, built in 1088. Rich Patmian sea captains, trading grain with Egypt, Russia and Italy in the 18th century, erected imposing residences with construction materials and furnishings imported from Europe.

In Symi, Kastelorizo and Halki neo-classicism brought a new sophistication; the stylish residences lining the waterfront, practically floating on the sea, were built in the 19th century when the islanders traded sea sponges even as far as the Americas. Pale ochre-hued façades decorated with pilasters, pediments and door knockers stand alongside unpretentious houses belonging to fishermen and herders.

The capital Rhodes has been one of the Mediterranean's most significant ports since ancient times. Within the old city four peoples – Greeks, Venetians, Franks and Turks – have left traces of the ideal each had conceived of life. Today, the medieval town preserves the striking appearance the Knights of St John bestowed upon it. Imposing palaces, wide, cobbled roads, which once echoed with the sound of the knights' horses' hooves, mosques, minarets, Byzantine domes and narrow streets with myriad surprises comprise this impressive town, an amalgam of civilizations.

Aegean architecture, the extension of ancient and Byzantine architecture, represents the Greeks' ideals: their deep religious faith, their belief in the family, their love of their homeland and tradition. It is the pure expression of the civilization of a people inextricably intertwined with the sea, a people who had an open view of the world beyond and always wanted to bring it home.

THE DODECANESE

between the sea and the sky

Twenty-five years ago Marcello Monezi and his Greek wife Katerina, then a young couple, happened upon the isle of Astypalaia. One August night, as their ship neared the island, they made out bright pinpoints of light like stars floating on the horizon. The steep bastions of the medieval fortress gradually started to gain shape in the darkness and the whitewashed domes of the churches and the cubic Aegean houses surrounding them glowed in the starlight. The Monezis loved the island at once: the simple lifestyle suited them perfectly and they have spent several summers here. Initially they bought a plot of land on a beach. It had a small hut, but because the only access was by boat they acquired a *tholari* (domed room) in Chora, the only village on the island. This was the first in a series of small houses the couple have bought on the 'oddly shaped rock'. The *tholari* has become the Monezis' beautiful white home, magnificent in its austerity and simplicity.

The summertime *meltemia* whistle through the narrow streets of the island village. Everything is blue and white – the white village throws its doors open wide to the blue Aegean. Behind the village rises a 13th-century Venetian fortress which belonged to the Quirini family for three hundred years until the arrival of the fearsome pirate Barbarosa. Up until the 19th century the island inhabitants lived within the walls of the fortress due to pirate raids and the *tholaria* were used as stables.

FAR LEFT The door leading to the garden is typical of the Dodecanese style.
LEFT The original pinewood front door.
TOP A basket of pomegranates grown in the grounds.
ABOVE A large earthenware jar in which olive oil was once stored.
OPPOSITE, LEFT The lack of space on the Dodecanese prompted the inhabitants to build their houses so that the roof of one could be the patio for the house above it. On the hill rises the 13th-century medieval castle of the Venetian Quirini family, with the orthodox chapel of the Virgin Mary.
OPPOSITE, ABOVE, RIGHT; AND BELOW, RIGHT The wooden balcony with a latticework railing is typical of Astypalaia.

When the danger of pirates passed, the *tholaria* were converted into houses, one for every family.

The Monezi house consists of three high-ceilinged *tholaria* – 10 metres (32 ft) in length and 3.5 metres (11½ ft) in width, each in the traditional style of the island with Greek *sofas* (beds raised on hand-carved stilts) skirting the room. The *tholaria* are joined internally by arches and externally by a common courtyard. The first *tholari* is the sitting room and kitchen, the second is Marcello's study and the third is the guestroom. An opening that resembles a well leads to the floor where the bedrooms and a small kitchen are located. A multi-level terrace crowns the whole complex.

The restoration of the house was a long and laborious affair due to a dearth of local restorers. Built of local stone with limestone lintels, the house sports split doors, allowing the top or bottom half to stay closed while the other opens, and latticed wooden balconies. As with all the local houses, there are openings only on the façade which keeps the building cool in the summer and warm in the winter.

The naval room in the first of the *tholari* is splashed with bright colours in tones of blue and green, while the rest of the house is in muted pastel tones. The sitting room floor is made of stone; ceramic tile from the traditional ceramists in Patmos covers the study floor, while the bedroom floors are pine.

As for the decoration, the Monezis opted for a look governed by the frugality of summer holidays: built-in couches, low tables and wood-carved shelves, skirting the walls, laden with peasant plates and jugs.

The whole house offers a stunning view of the entire northwestern side of the island and the ubiquitous blue of the doors and windows marries perfectly with the sunlight of the Aegean, all contributing to the charm of the original house.

OPPOSITE The small kitchen in between the upstairs bedrooms is useful on winter nights. The bench conceals the staircase spiralling down to the ground floor.

RIGHT A corner of the *tholari* which has more than one use to save space. The raised *sofas* reached by the steps are for sleeping and the built-in benches are for relaxing next to the circular, sculpture-like fireplace.

ABOVE The kitchen and sitting room are housed in a *tholari* 10 metres (32 ft) in length. This would once have been a whole house. The shelves skirting the walls, laden with ceramic plates, add a touch of local colour.

NEAR RIGHT The carved *grizzola* shelf from Astypalaia hosts kitchen utensils.

FAR RIGHT A kitchen cupboard made by a local carpenter.

ABOVE Marcello Monezi's study, decorated
in green and blue like a Greek fishing
boat, sports naval maps, a hydrometer and
compasses. It features built-in cupboards,
niches, a shelf with Dodecanese plates and
floor tiles handmade by a Patmian artisan.
The door leads to the bathroom and above it
there is another *sofa* for an occasional guest.

BELOW, LEFT A wooden basin stand painted the typical blue.

RIGHT Resplendent with light, simplicity and pastel tones, the high-ceilinged upstairs bedroom has a wooden floor and painted ceiling. It is furnished with a wooden carved bed and an Italian washstand.

BELOW, RIGHT The staircase was chiselled out of stone.

FAR RIGHT The six-metre (20-ft) high *tholari* has enough space to accommodate raised *sofas*. Small windows and thick stone walls provide protection from the heat.

in the shadow of the monastery

Patmos has always been a holy place. In around AD 95 St John the Apostle, exiled from Ephesus in Turkey, wrote the Book of Revelation on this tiny Dodecanese island. The main town of Chora, in the protective embrace of the 11th-century Monastery of St John, was not pillaged by conquerors and pirates, unlike the surrounding islands, so both the architecture and the population remained purely Greek. The white houses spread out from the high monastery walls, comprising the best-preserved Byzantine settlements in the whole of the Aegean.

A maze of narrow, identical streets – built thus to discourage potential invaders – have a succession of doors which disorientate the visitor. One of these doors, topped with a Byzantine cross on the stone lintel, leads to Tetty and Vasilis Stimfaliades' home. They first visited Patmos as a young couple in the 1970s on a quest to find a remote paradise. They were infatuated with the island's mystical atmosphere – 'an island forgotten by time'. They had already spent several summers on Patmos when someone showed them 'the house with the painted ceilings'. At that time the owner was not prepared to sell, but they persisted, asking every year until he suddenly changed his mind.

While crossing the courtyard, with its niches and benches, a cool breeze envelops you. The jasmine climbs the high, whitewashed walls. Once the residence of an archimandrite, the house is a typical example of Patmian Byzantine architecture. The Stimfaliades consider themselves heirs to an estate that does not belong to them, but was bestowed upon them so they could preserve it and pass it on intact to those who will succeed them.

A painter in her own right, Tetty adores the nostalgic atmosphere of the house and the only alterations she has made have been the addition of two bathrooms. The old plasterwork, the thick pine ceiling beams, the typical Patmian floor tiles and the windows and doors were all respectfully repaired and restored. However, the house had previously undergone a great number of architectural alterations and extensions over the years. Originally a cube-shaped, one-room house it was extended – probably in the 17th century – and later the second floor was added, with a small balcony and a staircase leading to it. A small house above the arch over the narrow street was also built. Today this is a guesthouse. Tetty did much restoration work, but with such a delicate touch that few would guess at the months of re-structuring involved.

The rooms still function in the same way as in the past. The ground floor, with a kitchen and covered courtyard, is the living area, while the first floor, with its towering ceilings, remains the place where guests are received. The bedroom and its built-in wooden bed are at the back.

The furnishings are typical of Patmian manor houses with collectibles acquired over the years from local houses and antique shops: mirrors from Patmos, ivory inlaid trunks from Syria, a brass four-poster bed from the island of Chios, a divan from northern Greece and kilims from Turkey. The walls host old portraits and Tetty's artwork, which reflects the constant inspiration of the sea beneath the terrace.

Here, the northerly winds whistle through the narrow streets as the thick clouds of fog bear down on the fortress-like monastery that looms in the background. Perhaps it was this fog that inspired St John the Apostle to pen his stirring Book of Revelation, 'and the moon became as blood; And the stars of heaven fell unto the earth, even as a fig tree casteth her untimely figs, when she is shaken of a mighty wind.' The guests enjoy perhaps the most beautiful view of the Aegean. The golden evening light paints the white level roofs of Chora a deep orange. Beyond them the scattered islands of Icaria, Leipsoi, Leros and Kalymnos emerge from the emerald waters to take on the coppery colours of the sunset.

OPPOSITE, ABOVE, LEFT The garden with
hibiscus and jasmine plants provides
welcome shade.

OPPOSITE, BELOW, RIGHT The small, quaint
kitchen has an old dish rack on the wall.

ABOVE A white stone bench and a few
cushions is all you need to find yourself
suspended between the blue of the Aegean
sea and the sky.

RIGHT Now a place to relax with a view of the
fortress monastery of St John Theologos and
the white houses of Chora, the terrace once
served to collect precious rainwater.

LEFT The *kalospito*, a typical Patmian salon, is a room within a room. Tetty Stimfaliades retained the 18th-century atmosphere by keeping the old doors, windows and painted ceilings, which are complemented by imported furniture such as the Syrian ivory inlaid chest.

BELOW The decorated mirror framing a corner of the salon probably arrived on the ship of a sea captain sailing home.

ABOVE Two aspects of the same narrow room located above the arch over the street. The room was built here to save space and was also a checkpoint for potential invasions. The floor is covered in handmade Patmian tiles and the Renaissance woman was painted by Tetty Stimfaliades.

OPPOSITE The high, brass bed came from the island of Chios.

neo-classical charm

As the ferry approaches Patmos, one's gaze travels upwards to the imposing medieval monastery, which looks more like a fortress than a house of prayer, crowning the island. Built in 1088 with permission of the Byzantine Emperor Alexis I Comnenus, the Monastery of St John (Agios Ioannis Theologos) is illuminated like a stage set, a fantastical backdrop to the bright white houses of the main town of Chora.

Enchanting, calm and mystic, Patmos attracts a cosmopolitan crowd – many of them eager to acquire one of its imposing residences. Greek designer Lea Raka Peratikou was one of them. Seventeen years ago she came to Patmos on holiday and instantly fell in love with the island. Well travelled, effervescent and energetic, she is famous for her glamorous parties in both Patmos and London. Apart from interiors, she also designs ceramics and fabrics, producing them according to the age-old techniques of the Dodecanese islands. Her Patmos home is tastefully decorated and designed so that she and

OPPOSITE, LEFT Long hallways with black and white tiles are a common feature in neo-classical houses.

OPPOSITE, RIGHT A family heirloom from Samos in the entrance hall.

ABOVE A large arch separates the hall from the staircase.

RIGHT The furnishings in the sitting room re-create the atmosphere of an old sea captain's house. The furniture is elegant and sophisticated with period pieces like the ones the captains used to bring back from Europe – an English sofa table, a French clock and a Corfiot commode with a Queen Anne mirror.

her family can live there in comfort four months of the year and entertain some of her jetsetting friends.

The white house rises up in one of the narrow labyrinthine streets leading to the monastery. Its interior is an oasis of serenity and coolness – the strong sunrays are tempered in the enclosed shaded courtyard and transformed into soft beams of silver light. Built in the late 19th century, the building seems to have more in common with neo-classicism than with a typical cubic Patmian structure. One of the most distinctive features of the high-rise two-storey house is the limestone lintels around the doors and windows, which have been engraved with a Byzantine cross – the island's emblem.

Like other houses in the neighbourhood, this one belonged to a wealthy family of sea captains – the Palaiologos family, who in the late 19th century were involved in the cotton and grain trade with Alexandria, Odessa and Venice. They travelled the world and wished to emulate the architectural elements and styles they had observed on their journeys in Europe. The neo-classical style with its large, comfortable spaces suited their temperament.

They decorated their home with English and French furnishings – Venetian mirrors, priceless icons, silver tea services – and employed the best Cretan painters and wood engravers.

The cosy reception area, with its ochre-tinted walls and floor laid with black and white, turn-of-the-20th-century tiles, leads via a spiral staircase to the first floor. The large living and dining room, with its many windows and all-encompassing view, is painted in bright sage colours like the sea and sky, bringing the colours of the horizon into the house. In this vast room even the soaring ceilings, the doors and the wooden floor are the colour of the sky. The old stone fireplace was once the cooking hearth when the room was used as a kitchen. The high, wood-planked ceilings throughout the house are also blue like the sky. The charm of this unusual home – furnished with period pieces, significant paintings and local finds – is a welcome contrast to the simplicity of the exterior.

At the end of the long corridor, the old well divides the reception areas from the kitchen and cellar – the older part of the house dating back to

the 17th century which has a more folklorish style with thick chestnut ceiling beams and Patmian cotto tiles on the floor. The interior wooden staircase continues up to the first floor, where there is a long hallway with bedrooms on either side, a feature of neo-classical architecture. The master bedroom, which has a view across the village, is painted in grey-green tones and sports a local latticework wardrobe. The large bathroom is decorated in azure sky-like tones. On the back wall of the house, flush against the mountain rock, two bedrooms, stencilled in sea shades, are furnished with the typical Greek *sofa* – a raised bed with a railing, a distinctive feature of the Dodecanese, which is used to save space.

Outside, the enclosed garden, with its high wall protecting it from northern winds and the curious eyes of thousands of people visiting the monastery, is the perfect place for an ouzo and a side dish. The house guests can sip and nibble on the white, terraced levels to the sound of the religious chants carried by the breeze from the monastery, while the scent of the surrounding jasmine, geraniums and blubayio tickles their nostrils.

ABOVE Exuding the cosmopolitan air of the island, the wall dividing the sitting room from the dining area is decorated with a series of traditional plates from Thrace.

RIGHT The bathroom combines local wooden latticework with white marble. The glass partitions off the shower, allowing the light to stream in.

BELOW The Greek *sofas*, raised beds with railings, are a distinctive, space-saving piece of furniture found all over the Dodecanese.

FAR RIGHT The English-style master bedroom has a grand four-poster bed; the mistress's desk overlooks the village of Chora.

enticing eastern air

Castles, palaces, gothic houses, monuments and imposing churches are elements of Rhodes's unique architectural style that have changed little over the past five centuries. The Italian Giuseppe Sala was seduced to such an extent that on his first visit to the island he bought a house. He did not opt for a place on one of the enchanting beaches, but for a home in the centre of the old town, on a street where up until a few years ago there were Turkish baths and red lights went on at night. Agiou Phanouriou Street is one of the most distinctive in the maze of the old town's criss-crossing cobbled roads. In the basement of the church, after which the street is named, a special type of pie called *phanouropita*, smelling sweetly of roasted chestnuts dipped in red wine and

BELOW Bright colours, rugs woven by the Berbers of northern Africa, copper pots and old local furniture have revived the Ottoman air of the house. The soaring ceilings, the ceiling beams, the floor made of 150-year-old Lebanese cedar and the staircase with the hatchway were all painstakingly preserved.
OPPOSITE, ABOVE The house is on a narrow street in the old town of Rhodes. The neo-classical-style door has a knocker in the shape of a hand.

cloves, is distributed among the church-goers every morning.

Between the successive arches lining the cobbled streets, where the craftsmen ply their trade – welding metal or tooling leather – rises Sala's enchanting house. The two-storey construction with arches and a spacious interior courtyard, laid with a pebblestone mosaic of the sun (the god of Rhodes), stands proudly in the Turkish quarter, dating from the 15th century when it was built during the time of the Knights of St John of Jerusalem. The plain exterior gives little away, but inside is a unique sample of a knightly urban residence with Ottoman and medieval influences, dazzling colours and an oriental air.

A cosmopolitan nomad and artist, Sala has an intuitive gift for creating very special homes. He divides his time between his houses in Milan, Rio de Janeiro and his beloved Rhodes.

A cool breeze envelops the visitor upon entering the large hall with arches that support the main building. A wooden staircase leads to the first floor where there is a spacious salon around which the other rooms are located. Wandering through the house, one discovers that the various conquerors of the island added on architectural features that remained untouched over the centuries, creating an astounding fusion. The exterior stone walls are high and austere to keep out invaders and date back, as do the arches, to the time of the Knights of St John of Jerusalem. The Turks later added the latticed windows and the Greeks introduced neo-classical elements such as the main door with the door knocker dating from 1900. The oblong extension to the main building was constructed in 1950 to meet the residents' needs for bathrooms on the first floor and a kitchen on the ground floor.

BELOW, LEFT **In the lush interior courtyard, the pebbled pavement depicts the sun god of Rhodes.**
BELOW, MIDDLE **A watercolour by Giuseppe Sala.**
BELOW, RIGHT **The Turkish bath, converted into the main bathroom, is where water, light and pampering are the essential players.**

ABOVE, LEFT **A plate rack brimming with 1930s Italian porcelain; the kitchen is decorated in ochre tones.**

ABOVE, RIGHT **Harmonious colours and windows overlooking the interior courtyard are features of the new extension to the house.**

OPPOSITE **The counter in front of the kitchen is ideal for outdoor cooking in the summer.**

During the period of Ottoman rule the house was known as a *serai* – a wealthy residence. The tenants lived on the ground floor and the owners on the first floor. Sala bought the house, imagining himself to be a wealthy Turk in the late 18th century. He collected furniture and crystal from Europe and fabrics and *objets d'art* from the local shops, and the North African and Turkish bazaars – as the Turks did – and fabrics and rugs from the East. The end result is a house that brims with passion and sensuousness, where English velvets and gauzes, Italian brocades, Indian silks, Greek cotton weaves, bone china, family heirlooms, gravures and African Berber carvings co-exist harmoniously. Whatever Sala was not able to find in the antique markets, he designed himself and had the local carpenters make for him. As you would find in a Turkish home, he coloured the walls with washes of deep red, blue, green and ochre, and chose brightly coloured furnishings.

When undertaking the restoration Sala was concerned with retaining the most significant features of the house. On the first storey he kept the floors, made of a special type of highly durable Lebanese cedar called *katrani* which came from Asia Minor 150 years ago. The six-metre (20-ft) high ceilings are constructed from solid wood cross beams. In times past there would have been a wooden *sofa* that allowed the Muslim women to climb up and watch the goings on of the street from behind small lattice windows with tiny apertures – these meant they could not be seen by passers by. As was once common practice in the Aegean, the roof is made of *patilia*, compact mud that has to be renewed every year. Sala preferred to keep this type of roof even though a drop or two of rain might seep through during the winter. The jewel of the house is the old Turkish bath – the main bathroom of the house – painted ochre and domed with small slit openings that allow the sun beams to pierce through.

The courtyard, visible from all the rooms of the house, has cheerful patterns and features the colours of the Aegean and brings its benevolent breeze and the scents of the jacaranda, bougainvillaea and pomegranate trees. It no wonder this is the owner's favourite hiding place where, in the shade of the trees, he loves to sketch and paint watercolours of, naturally, his beloved Rhodes.

LEFT The deep Byzantine red décor and the gauzy curtains languidly draped around the Italian wrought-iron bed create a sensual atmosphere. The tiny windows at the top once allowed the Ottoman women to look out onto the street without being seen by passers by.

bold dodecanese style

In Lindos's maze of winding streets the only clue to the existence of the Clow house is a simple, almost hidden door in a high, whitewashed garden wall. Upon crossing the threshold and going through the medieval arched stone tunnel at the far end one finds a cool oasis of lush greenery. The courtyard, which is used for dining in the summer, is laid with pebblestone motifs from Byzantine and Greek popular art and is the soul of the house.

Built in the 17th century by a wealthy seafarer, the manor house is an example of Lindian architecture – that singular blend of Byzantine, medieval and Ottoman elements – and has a fascinating history. Seated in the courtyard, Mary Clow, the mistress of the house, reminisces and tells of the house's history. In the 1890s the owners entertained the first archae-ologist to excavate ancient Lindos, a German baron.

Mary Clow recounts the interesting story of her late husband, who fell in love with Lindos just as she had done. In 1960 a romantic, sophisticated New Yorker named Bill Clow, overwhelmed by the beauty and purity of the place, dared to live alone without plumbing and electricity. In those days Lindos was grindingly poor – there were no jobs and the young men emigrated to Australia, Canada and Germany, leaving behind their weeping brides and babies. Clow was moved by their hardship and revived an ancient hand-weaving tradition, setting up 'The Looms of Lindos'. He employed twenty young girls who worked for their marriage dowries and created unique handi-work sold all over the world. This was the biggest enterprise for miles around and it continued for twenty years until tourism took over and the island of Rhodes became one of the most prosperous in Greece.

ABOVE, LEFT A hanging lamp from the East suspended in the stone arched tunnel that leads to the courtyard.
ABOVE, MIDDLE The sofa in the *sala* is the perfect place to snuggle with one of Bill Clow's numerous books. The two windows at the top provide light and ventilation.
ABOVE, RIGHT The striking painted ceiling in the *sala* is made of solid wooden beams and dates back to the 17th century.
OPPOSITE Filled with folk works of art and laid with pebbles, the large living room is typical of Lindos. It is divided into two areas connected by a vaulted arch. The benches, the bed on a platform and the bridal chest are all covered with local cotton or wool fabrics hand woven on a loom.

The main house is a towering block built on two levels in an L-shape overlooking a courtyard. A stone staircase leads up to 'The Captain's Room' – as the locals call it – which sports a series of windows and a balcony with a view of the Lindos Acropolis. The *sala*, or living room, with its massive stone arch supporting the magnificent painted ceiling, original in every detail, is one of the finest examples of genuine Lindian architecture. The floor is laid in black and white pebbles which creates beautiful patterns, while the main door, windows and skylights mean the *sala* has proper ventilation and is well lit.

In past times the *sala* was particularly important when there was a bride in the family. The upper platform was then adorned with special curtains of hand-woven silk, embroidered lace and cotton-weave fabrics dyed deep red, blue and leaf green. The bride and bridegroom sat behind the curtains, the bride in a traditional, loom-woven costume embroidered with treasures handed down through generations (today, some such costumes are on exhibit in the Rhodes museum). All around the couple sat guests singing mantinades, accompanied by music played on traditional instruments. The wedding reception would become increasingly livelier all through the night and very often continued into the next day and even the day after.

Throughout the Aegean, one-room houses have a fireplace in one corner for warmth and simple cooking. In this house the fireplace is in the 'winter room', which is next to the *sala* through a wooden double door. A very cosy room with a *sofa*, this is where the family used to play cards in front of a wood fire in the winter. The *sofa* has a secret – covered by rugs and cushions, a small trap-door drops into an enclosed, windowless room, whitewashed and with a pebble floor. In the old days a secret room was especially useful for storing food supplies and for hiding children in the event of invasions.

When Mary Clow bought the house it had never been modernized – all she did was install plumbing and electricity, add an extra bathroom and whitewash the smooth surfaces and the plaster mouldings around the *sala* windows. In contrast to the rest of the house, Mary painted the bedrooms in bright colours. Outside, the chiselled stone remains unplastered and so the sunlight creates a chiaroscuro effect that softens the glare of the sunlight. The kitchen is a pleasant surprise, tucked away in a lush corner of the courtyard: a domed room, cool and spacious, painted in traditional Greek periwinkle blue. Mary was delighted to be able to set a panel of her husband's collection of Persian tile fragments in the kitchen wall and floor.

All the rooms have Ottoman-style built-in wooden platforms (*sofas*) and benches (*pangous*) built around the perimeter and covered with rugs and embroidered cushions. They are used for sleeping or sitting and provide copious storage space underneath. They suit the Clows' lifestyle, allowing for any number of unexpected guests and children. Other pieces include bridal jewelry, hand-made tables and café chairs from the village, which make up the simple and unpretentious furniture. A collection of distaffs, hand-painted dishes, local ceramics and cotton and wool fabrics woven on the looms complement the house's atmosphere which is so decidedly Greek.

OPPOSITE, LEFT An exterior staircase links the courtyard to 'The Captain's Room'.

OPPOSITE, MIDDLE In the late afternoon, after a day on the beach, the cool shade of the trees in the summer dining area is a godsend.

OPPOSITE, RIGHT Large earthenware jugs that were once used to store olive oil now host begonias and geraniums in the courtyard.

ABOVE Washed in the traditional indigo blue, the kitchen is a separate room in the courtyard. The plate rack between the oven and the Persian tiles is filled with Rhodian ceramics.

RIGHT An old distaff for spinning wool is now used as a tea towel rack.

OPPOSITE The 'winter room' has a platform with twin beds covered with local hand-woven bedspreads. The staircase leads up to a bedroom. The Ottoman-style fireplace is topped by a shelf displaying traditional decorative plates.

ABOVE The *sofas* in the large *sala* have embroidered pillowcases and cotton mattresses which were of great significance in times past. Adorned with special curtains on wedding days, this is where the bride and groom would sit surrounded by their guests, who sang folk songs and danced to the accompaniment of traditional instruments.

a medieval noble's house

In the early 1960s a young Italian painter travelling through the Aegean set eyes on Lindos's white houses tumbling down the mountainside towards the sea. That was enough – not long afterwards he acquired a house that became for him (and later for his family) a beloved, restful summer retreat.

It is almost impossible to wade through the waves of tourists flooding the countless streets of Lindos in the summer. But the arches and the heavy, wooden, nail-studded doors – some painted blue or green and some letting the natural wood show through – lead to shady courtyards. Pushing one of these open, the visitor finds himself under a unique dome with a cross-vaulted roof. The hum of the crowd is immediately muffled; a blessed cool calmness envelops the lush, green courtyard.

Surrounded by buildings made of local limestone, the imposing main house, the medieval-style building with a 'harem' room and the square, tall tower all exude the glory of the age of knighthood. Series of vaulted arches, suspended corridors, a covered balcony with columns and sun-washed terraces connect the buildings. The floors are laid in pebblestones, called *hohlakia* here. They are set in patterns of dolphins, the Greek key and flowers inspired by popular Byzantine and Greek motifs.

Over four hundred years old, this house, with its thick stone walls, is a blend of Dodecanese, Byzantine, medieval and Ottoman architecture. The dominating front door bears testimony to the history of the house – it is Arabic in shape and carved out of the limestone in relief are a Byzantine double-headed eagle, rosettes and a cross. Braid-like patterns symbolizing infinity – the same type that can be seen on local Minoan pottery – also surround the door. Alongside is a carving of St George slaying the dragon. One can make out the inscribed date of 1666, which means the house was built in the period of domination by the Knights of St John. These symbols have led the locals to believe that the house once belonged to an Ecumenical Patriarch, perhaps Ioanikios of Lindos, who lived here in the 16th century.

During the difficult 1960s when times were hard, the owners had the foresight to commission the help of the great Athenian architect Nikos Hatzimichalis. With dedication and respect he renovated the place – apart from creating bathrooms and a kitchen, the house remained essentially true to itself. The local artisans, headed by Filipis Filipou, revived the beautiful architectural elements with talent and artistry. Preserved throughout the centuries, the house is a rare example of local architecture.

Upon entering via the studded, wooden door, one is faced with a large room which has a superb high, painted wooden ceiling, interrupted by a large arch. The black and white pebbled floor is ideal for the easy, informal holiday lifestyle of the Italian owners. A smaller arch leads to the dining area. The furniture is sparse, subtle and simple, combining disparate Rhodian and European pieces that produce a sophisticated local look. Locally bought wooden chests dating from the 18th century, old ceramics and wooden *sofas* coexist with English colonial leather armchairs, Spanish dining room furniture and African wall panels. Wood, stone, pebble, old Italian and traditional Rhodian ceramic tiles are now, as then, the favoured decorative materials.

From the entrance hall a steep wooden staircase leads to various levels and subsequent extensions, where narrow passageways, secret hideaways, corridors and niches exude an air of medieval mystery. At the top of another even narrower and creakier wooden staircase a surprise awaits: the harem room. In the dimness created by the handmade straw curtains one can just make out the wooden latticework that covers the walls of both rooms. The awe-inspiring craftsmanship is perhaps the best preserved in all of the Aegean. Outside, the balcony, its roof supported by columns, offers a limitless view of the village and the sea – one no doubt enjoyed by the Ottoman wives who once sat there. A narrow passageway leads to the tower that is a guestroom today.

Whenever possible, the Italian owners make the time to find refuge here and enjoy the comforts of their manor house. In the morning, under the shady trees, they indulge in the coolness; in the evening, while relaxing on comfortable cushions on the terrace, they watch the blazing sun dip into the warm Aegean. This is when the sea breeze scatters the intoxicating scent of the exotic frangipane.

OPPOSITE With beautiful columns, the medieval balcony overlooks the courtyard. It dates back to the time of the Knights of St John.

BELOW Centuries of history are reflected in the stone-carved entrance. The Minoan braids symbolize infinity, the two-headed eagle, the rosettes and the cross are Byzantine, while the shape of the door is Arabic in origin.

RIGHT The Lindian living room with superb high wooden ceilings, a large arch and a white pebbled floor leads to the courtyard. English colonial leather armchairs, African hide wall panels and old Rhodian ceramic pots create a sophisticated look.

RIGHT Carefully renovated by the owners, the harem room is perhaps the best preserved in all of the Aegean. Its amazing wood-carved latticework, the cupboards and the decorative niches are echoed in the smaller adjacent room.

OPPOSITE, ABOVE A cheerful atmosphere in the tower guestroom. The wooden beds, the table and the door and window frames are new, but were crafted by local artisans.

OPPOSITE, BELOW, LEFT Between the tower with the singular chimney stack and the columned balcony on the first floor, there is a small terrace overlooking the narrow street on one side and the courtyard on the other.

OPPOSITE, BELOW, RIGHT The medieval balcony window in the tower is framed by stone-carved braids like those on ancient urns.

ABOVE A succession of arches made of local limestone in the shower cubicle.

RIGHT Simplicity reigns in the bathroom with a traditional wooden beam and cane ceiling. The counter, with Rhodian tiles, sports two copper basins.

harmonizing styles

The Grazias, an Italian couple, were sailing through the Aegean on their boat when they happened upon the picturesque port of Symi one afternoon. One look was enough: they had to buy a house on the island.

According to Greek myth, Symi was the King of Rhodes's daughter and Glaucus snatched her from her homeland and brought her to this barren and deserted island. Symi is predominantly rocks, clear turquoise waters, hidden coves, monasteries and neo-classical houses sprayed by the waves, but Chorio, inhabited since antiquity and the highest point of the island's settlement which overlooks the port and the neighbouring islands, is also located here. It once sported a fortress surrounded by houses and later the wealthy Symian merchants and captains chose to build their tremendously luxurious residences here so they could keep a watchful eye on the sea and their ships.

The origins of the Grazia house lie in the mid-18th century when the successful captain and ship-owner Diakidis built a home for his family. During the Italian Occupation his descendants transformed the well-protected ground floor into a secret school where the neighbouring children learned their mother tongue. The house had always belonged to the same family up until the 1990s when the Grazias were enchanted by its unexpected architectural features.

The Gothic arches, the vaulted loggias, the tiled roof, the pebbled terraces and patios and, most importantly, the ingenious use of different openings to protect from the furious wind all originate from both the East and West. This amalgam of features is not to be found in other houses in the area and it is this originality that intrigued the Grazias. The couple realized that renovating the house was going to be a great undertaking, so they commissioned Anastasia Papaioannou, an architect who has been responsible for the design of almost ninety houses on the island. Living here for a great part of the year, she is sensitive to the local architecture and instinctively understands what can and cannot be done within the island's building tradition – the house won the 1999 Europa Nostra Architecture Award for the best renovation of the year.

ABOVE, LEFT The kitchen, with its table from an
Athenian antique shop, and handmade blue and
white tiles and wall lantern from Rhodes, stayed
where it had always been, on the ground floor.
ABOVE, RIGHT In the sitting room the hanging
church lamp and the kilim all bear the
characteristic colours of Symi. The floor was
created by mixing cement with burgundy dye.
OPPOSITE Previously the cooking area, the ground
floor is in the style of the local architecture. The
sofas between the wooden columns made of tree
trunks were constructed by a local carpenter, as
was the ceiling.

The architect did not wish to change anything in the structure and shape of the house, except to adapt it to modern living conditions. It had seen many modifications – such as doors with ornaments and engravings, framed windows, wooden balconies with ironwork – due to the neo-classical aesthetic that predominated in Symi in the late 19th century.

The courtyard has loggias and a small exterior staircase which leads to the large veranda, with arches, on the first floor; on the other side of the house through the entrance is the ground-floor kitchen cum sitting room, where the auxiliary cooking areas once were. A small interior staircase leads to the next floor which used to be the main house and is now where the bedrooms are located. This is why each floor has a different architectural style – the low-ceilinged and rather dark spaces on the ground floor contrast with the high-ceilinged, spacious and bright rooms on the first floor. This singularity turned out to be to the dwellers' advantage as Symi is known for its warm climate and it is very soothing, after a day at the beach, to enter the cool kitchen cum sitting room and have a siesta on the large traditional *sofas*, which also double as a partition.

What appears to be a simple Symian holiday home on the ground floor, with the sitting room arranged in traditional style: bright colours, tree trunks, painted cement floors, thick rafters and Greek rustic furnishings, contrasts with the European style of the first floor with its high ceilings, wooden floors and minimalist style. The result effectively merges island tradition with Eastern-style charm.

At dusk on the large veranda there is an air of languidness – not a single wave ripples the sea; the breeze is warm with the intoxicating scent of pine needles. Nothing stirs apart from the fishermen in their caïques on their way to cast their nets, as they have always done over the centuries. No wonder their Turkish neighbours call the Symian people *Sibekili*, 'fast-travelling': they used to build some of the fastest boats in the Mediterranean – a striking contrast to the slow pace of life on Symi today.

colours from paradise

Like a shard of rock, Symi rises up from the bright
blue sea. Just a few nautical miles from Turkey,
this microscopic isle in the southeasternmost part
of the Aegean emanates a charm all its own. The
island is not just made up of the blues of the sea and
sky, but also the town Chorio which clings to the
rock and has an impressive neo-classical style.

'We had arrived on the ferryboat at six in the
morning. Ever since that day we have been back
unfailingly for the past twelve years.' The highest
point of the port is the spot Barbara and Carlo
Badin chose for their summerhouse, defying the
hundreds of steps one must climb to get there
from the port of Yialos. Built at the turn of the
20th century in a region where the shepherds milked
their sheep and goats, the fortress-shaped house
commands a panoramic view of the whole northwestern part of the island.

Anastasia Papaioannou undertook the architectural
renovation and remodelling. The small size perfectly
suited the family's needs and so she did not make
any changes to the structure – a one-room house,
typical of the local village-style architecture, with
a bedroom partitioned off by a wooden panel, and
a staircase on the side. At the top there is a wooden
platform that creates an interior balcony looking
over the rest of the room. The balcony was designed
from scratch by the architect, as was the built-in
wooden couch running round the parameter under
the windows – both are features found in most
houses in Symi. The kitchen is a separate room
that was once connected to the main house by the
courtyard, while today there is an interior door
linking the two buildings.

The renovation was carried out by local artisans
who used very few modern materials. Everything
had to be loaded onto donkeys and brought up from
the port. Old boards were converted into doors;
mismatched tiles dressed the kitchen wall and the

shower cubicle; the sitting room floor was comprised of a combination of brick and wood; cane thatched the roof covering the veranda; the walls were washed with the colours of the sun and sky; and ochre-coloured plaster was slapped onto the exterior walls.

Barbara is a stylist and craftswoman, while Carlo is a set designer. As artists, they wanted a small, cheerful and functional holiday home: their main aim was to fill it with light and colour so they could enjoy it with their children. In fact, decorating the place was a family affair. Barbara painted the kitchen walls with stripes, crafted picture frames in a mosaic of glass and stones, made cushions and wove cool fabrics on the small loom in the loft. Old furniture and window shutters came to life in Carlo's hands with coats of vivid paint. Even the children lent a hand: little Katerina and Marco painted the picture that adorns the loft wall as well as their beds and chairs. But colour is the key element in the decoration since as Barbara says, in Symi, 'you walk along coloured streets'. The outcome is a truly happy household, brimming with colour and vitality.

Dinner takes place at dusk on the veranda. When Barbara lights the lanterns and candles, the atmosphere becomes magical, with the landscape of Symi under the starry sky as the perfect backdrop.

OPPOSITE Before setting off for the beach, little Katerina poses on the veranda next to the chair she painted with her brother Marco. The old Symi house with red-washed stone walls against sea-blue windows has taken on a new life under its present owners.
LEFT An old cupboard in the colourful kitchen houses the crockery. Barbara Badin stencilled the stripes on the wall. The doorway leads to the sitting room.

ABOVE, LEFT A typically Greek *kafenion*-style
table and wall niche cum bookcase.
ABOVE, RIGHT Gauzy curtains buffeting above
the built-in couch create a holiday atmosphere. The high ceilings and the windows
reveal the house's neo-classical origins.
OPPOSITE The loft is typical of the local
architecture. The architect employed the
colours one would find on a walk through
the narrow streets of Symi.

peace in pastel tones

Tiny, quiet and located at one of the southernmost points of the Aegean, Symi is a captivating island. Well hidden behind other islands and fjord-like peninsulas, it suddenly appears as though a curtain has opened on a stage set. More than two thousand houses surround the port in an amphitheatrical embrace.

Neo-classical-style houses in pastel tones adorn the port of Yialos. One of them belongs to a German newspaper editor and his wife who are long-time admirers of Symi and every summer cannot wait to finish dealing with their professional obligations and head south to their favourite island. East facing, tall,

informally elegant in Aegean neo-classical style, the house was built at the turn of the 20th century by a family of island notables; during the Second World War it operated as an army hospital. Painted in mellow Greek tones of blue, white and yellow, its most distinctive feature is the pediments on the roof and the smaller ones over the windows.

Two storeyed with a central corridor on the ground floor lined with rooms on either side, it has an interior, wooden staircase that leads to the first floor where the salon is located. This magnificent room, with its many windows and all-encompassing view, has soaring ceilings and wide-planked floors of durable pinewood imported from Turkey. The high windows and the French doors are one of the house's real advantages, allowing the Aegean light to flood in all day long and at sunset the sunbeams are refracted in a game of playful shadows. A calm atmosphere prevails – the result of pastel tones, light, breezy curtains and the few, select furnishings. Greek antiques from the early 20th century and Art Nouveau pieces such as the large living room mirror, which came with the house, happily sit side by side with the traditional *sofas* built by the local carpenter. They all conjure up the atmosphere of Greece.

The renovation was enjoyable, aided by the architect Anastasia Papaioannou, who was deeply respectful of the character of the urban-style home and did not attempt to make radical changes to the layout of the rooms. With particular care, the architect paid attention to each and every detail: she ordered the window grids from the local blacksmith, who copied the old design; she replaced the old, weather-worn window frames with new ones in exactly the same style; she retained most of the old panel doors inside. For the flooring on the ground floor she chose cotto tiles, attractively contrasting with the blue walls, while in the guestroom, the cotto tiles are

interspersed with hand-painted Italian tiles. One room is innovatively floored with slates and pebbles which have been inserted in the cement grouting, and the bathroom floor is laid with white marble from Dionysos.

A real oasis is the patio at the back that looks out over the village and the surrounding hills. It is paved in black and white pebbles in geometrical motifs and dotted with large earthenware pots, where grain and nuts were once stored. At the front of the house the view from the wooden balcony is magical. The lights from the port shine like fireflies; the small taverns serve fresh fish next to the waves breaking on the shore; the boats bob on the sea surface, while the moon glows benevolently overhead.

OPPOSITE, LEFT The façade of the house skirted by the pebblestone courtyard is typical of the local architecture.
OPPOSITE, ABOVE, RIGHT A local-style veranda at the back overlooks the rolling hills.
OPPOSITE, BELOW, RIGHT A relaxing niche with a couch beneath a map of Symi on the wall.
ABOVE The elegant salon where the sea breeze can be felt is furnished with an old dining room set and art nouveau mirror that came with the house.

OPPOSITE The house's neo-classical style is due to the wealthy merchants who brought new ideas from Europe. The high-ceilinged salon is in traditional pastel tones; the old doors and the floor made of Lebanese cedar imported from Asia Minor were preserved.

ABOVE, LEFT In the bathroom the latticework on the doors below the basins – constructed by a local carpenter – inspired the furnishings and the door. The counter is made of Dionysos marble.

ABOVE, RIGHT The *sofas* recall the blue sea and have useful storage space. The terracotta floor tiles are scattered with blue and white Italian tiles.

The southernmost island of the Aegean, Crete is the crossroads of three civilizations: European, Asian and African. During their 4,000-year history the Cretans have seen the collapse of the Minoan civilization, the expansionism of the Roman Empire, the rise of Venice, the Turkish slave markets and the mass tourism of today. The last Turk left the island in 1896 and Crete only ceded to Greece in 1913. Despite these influences, the houses are still built in the traditional way – the Palace of Phaestos in Knossos, the Byzantine churches, the Venetian castles and the mosques happily coexist with humble one-room houses.

Like a microcosm of Greece, Crete combines features such as rugged, 2,000-metre (6,500-ft) high rocky mountains, snow-capped even in June, hidden plateaus, flat-roofed villages baking in the midday sun, deep, endless gorges, plains full of secrets and white sandy beaches.

Irakleio, Hania and Rethymno, Minoan cities of Cretan naval dominance strategically located along the East–West sea route, bear the strong architectural traces of various conquerors. Irakleio, the homeland of El Greco, is a modern metropolis. Colourful, neo-classical houses can be found in the Venetian port of Hania. Strolling along the shaded, narrow streets among the towering houses behind the port, the mystical air and the dim light calm the sensibilities, the aroma of home cooking tickles your nose and the hand-woven linens airing on the balconies all make you forget the noisy crowd in the port just a few streets away. It is like a fantastical journey through time: fortresses with moats, Catholic cathedrals side by side with Russian Orthodox churches and synagogues, and the market stalls brimming with local delicacies. A Venetian fortress proudly governs Rethymno. In the narrow streets with wooden balconies, dating back to the times of Ottoman Rule, Venetian fountains, loggias and mosques tell of the city's fascinating history.

The simple village homes, built on two levels and with an arched front door, are surrounded by a high wall. Ever since Minoan times, olive oil, wine and cheese have been stored in large earthen-ware jars on the ground floor. One of the most characteristic features of the house is the *doma*, the flat roof – exactly like the ones in the Palace of Knossos – made of mud in the past, now of concrete, built so that the rainwater can drain off.

In the small mountain villages of Crete there are still labyrinths of winding streets with steps and intersections covered by arches. Cretan men in their fringed headbands and roomy trousers tucked into their high boots relax in the village squares. You can spy them stamping grapes in wine vats in their homes, raising the dust while wildly dancing to the Cretan lyre, drinking *tsikoudia* and singing Erotokritos (a 17th-century epic) for hours, their joie de vivre never flagging while they empty their shotguns into the air.

The olive groves cascade like waterfalls down the mountainsides next to the deep gorges over-looking the Libyan or Aegean Sea. This is the home of the Minotaur and Daedalus, it is the land of a mountain-dwelling and hospitable people, who breathe thyme-scented air and always have the tinkling of goat bells in their ears.

CRETE

a view of the sea

On the west coast of Crete, this house with its Venetian arches gazes defiantly out on the Mediterranean Sea. A keen sense of modernity and a respect for the natural environment have made a unique, restful retreat. The house harmoniously blends with the local architecture. The large arched entrance, leading to a small enclosed courtyard, revives memories of the Venetians who left their mark on the island.

With a panoramic view of Falasarna Bay – the ancient port, the sand dunes and the stretch of olive groves – the house is in a truly advantageous location. Here, the sounds of the sea mix with the tinkle of sheep bells and shepherds' chidings echoing from the surrounding hills. Liana and Yiorgos Arahovitis felt impelled to discover the old community after reading *Monumenti Veneti*

nell'isola di Creta (1905–1932) by Giuseppe Gerola. They were enchanted by the unspoilt village, the beautiful beach, the view of the sunset, the surrounding olive trees, but most of all by the two small, dilapidated 19th-century buildings and the neighbouring late 16th-century tower below.

The couple, both well-known Athenian architects with many great buildings to their credit, wanted to realize a dream that would combine an ancient and a modern vision.

The original house featured flat roofs and numerous arches; one building was in the shape of a fortress and the other was cubic. Stables divided the two buildings, but the architects cleverly joined them by putting the kitchen in between. The guesthouse was built at the end of the large veranda, protecting the house from the wild north-

western winds. The interior spaces are all in a line so each enjoys a view of the vast sea.

Colour, light, restful purity of line and the combination of old local features and materials with modern ones is apparent everywhere. Marble flagstone from Rhodes has been extensively used for the floors – it is unique because of its scattered cobalt inlays – while on the veranda, modern coloured tiles break the monotony of the grey stone.

The exterior walls, built of old sandstone, are plastered over in places although in others the stone peeks through. The walls facing the sea, however, are unplastered. Colour is one of the essential elements of the house – traditional ochre is mixed in with the plaster on the exterior, creating a contrast with the modern doors and window frames painted ocean blue. The sitting room is perfectly cosy with its

OPPOSITE A courtyard gives protection from the northwesterly winds. In the new buildings parts of the sandstone wall are unplastered.

ABOVE The large veranda opens on to Falasarna Bay and the sea beyond.

NEAR RIGHT The shady cane pergola provides relief from the sun overhead.

FAR RIGHT Two bedrooms are housed in the Venetian tower. The stone walls are plastered in the traditional way with a mixture of ochre pigment, lime and earth.

OVERLEAF, LEFT-HAND PAGE, LEFT The wooden staircase leading from the bedroom down to the ground floor is reinforced with metal.

LEFT-HAND PAGE, RIGHT In every corner the traditional and the contemporary go hand in hand with bright colours. The ultra modern kitchen designed by the architects is framed by an old stone arch.

RIGHT-HAND PAGE, ABOVE, LEFT A glass pane divides the bedroom from the stairwell.

RIGHT-HAND PAGE, BELOW, LEFT The architect transformed the old bread oven into a modern fireplace with a metal chimney.

RIGHT-HAND PAGE, RIGHT On the sitting room ceiling wooden beams are coupled with exposed concrete framed by beechwood.

earthy tones, and the ceiling stems directly from the blue sky and the solid Arahovitis-designed furniture is made of oak from the surrounding hills.

The contemporary ceiling of exposed concrete painted blue, framed by beechwood, sets the tone for the sitting room while the old wood stove in the corner recalls the origins of the house. The ultra modern kitchen has been decorated in bright blue and red, like the bathrooms, and the iron and wood staircase leading to the master bedroom is a modern touch that contrasts with the traditional exterior. This contrast between the traditional and the contemporary is the architects' trademark – for them the modern provides comfort and enjoyment.

A shady cane pergola and the cool sitting area in the centre of the large terrace give relief from the sun overhead. Here, the great Mediterranean Sea fills the view as far as the eye can see.

a ceramist's retreat

'Ta Lefka Ori. This great harp of rocks is a-dazzle with snow all winter – the chief peaks crowd up to over two thousand metres – and it spells the secrecy and silence which lie at the heart of the Cretan spirit, and thus the most likely nursery for Zeus. The whole western end of the island is dominated by them, all skylines bend to their whiteness, all ballad singers tune in their image.' This is how Lawrence Durrell describes the largest mountain range in Crete in his delightful travel book *The Greek Islands*. At the foot of the mountainous mass, the villages characteristically grow on hilltops, tucked away in the olive groves, vineyards and herb bushes. In this primordial place, where traditions hold fast and stand the test of time, farmers store their produce in large earthenware pots

in the cellars of their houses – a practice that dates back to Minoan times. These are the same type of pots one sees in the ancient sites of Phaestos, Malia and Eleutherna, where the oldest pottery ever was unearthed. Here, the ceramists' kilns burned night and day up until just a few years ago.

Manousos Halkiadakis was born in one of these villages, called Paidohori, not too far from the town of Hania, between the Aegean Sea and the Lefka Ori (White Mountains). As a teenager, Halkiadakis left the village, as Cretan boys often do, to make his fortune in the big city. He studied Economics and Political Science, but the art of ceramics won him over. Despite winning international awards and the fact that he had worked in the studios of famous

ceramists, after a few years he decided he wanted to escape the urban environment – after all, pure Cretan nature is an essential element of his artistic work. He chose to make his native land his home and bought an old house, nearly derelict, which surveys the sea, the snow-capped mountains and the stone houses from its hilltop niche.

The 150-year-old structure is immediately recognizable as a typically Cretan dwelling: Doric, distinguished and very proud. The thick, stone walls are built on different levels, creating terraces, staircases and benches. The house is surrounded by a large garden with fruit, nut and olive trees.

In renovating the place, architect Yiorgos Sologanis did not wish to make major alterations

OPPOSITE The chiselled cornerstones were left exposed on the veranda, while the walls were plastered according to an age-old technique.
LEFT A place to relax under the grapevines.
BELOW Little boats float on a platter; the large one at the bottom is destined for an international exhibition in Italy.
OVERLEAF, LEFT The dining room exudes an air of rusticity with its Cretan rough-hewn chairs and earthenware jugs, urns and platters scattered everywhere.
OVERLEAF, RIGHT Once outside in the courtyard, now the oven has become the heart of the house. The banquette covers were hand woven by Manousos Halkiadakis's grandmother.

to the interior layout of the house. The modifications were made with functionality and adaptation to modern needs in mind.

The amazing structural elements, such as the Cretan bread oven – the hearth of the home – and the slanted roof of cypress tree beams were used to their best advantage. The ground floor, where the earthenware pots used to be stored, became living areas, while the rooms on the first floor were converted into bedrooms. The oven, which used to be outside, was enclosed and became the central point of the house and the large chimney protruding from it pierces through the house up to the attic,

visible from the interior balconies. Traditional techniques were employed such as 'pressed plaster' for the walls (a mixture of lime, earth and ochre dye), the old wooden window frames were repaired and untreated wooden floors were laid on the first floor.

What Halkiadakis wanted most was to preserve the atmosphere of the old house. The furnishings are simple and tastefully arranged, some pieces are family heirlooms and others were bought from antique shops. His own basins, balls, platters, candelabras, boxes, huge model ships and also tiny archetypal forms and totally modern ones are characterized by a shiny surface that lends them a special glow.

All of Halkiadakis's pieces are unique and, scattered around the house, bring vitality and colour.

He works daily in the small workshop he set up in the garden – like the first ceramists of the region did 6,000 years ago. The house, surrounded by the enchanting landscape, inspired the artist to turn his back forever on the greyness of the city and rediscover the colour of his homeland: from the sea he took cobalt blue and emerald green; from the earth tones, ochre and from the sun, beige and yellows. 'I found myself here in the ever snowy Lefka Ori, the moon, the sea, the valley of olive trees, the locust trees and the scents of the earth.'

LEFT The cobalt blue hanging candelabra and sphere, made by Manousos Halkiadakis, set the tone in the sparing corner of the sitting room.

BELOW Using a layer of glass, Halkiadakis created a blinding turquoise blue ceramic basin in the garden.

BOTTOM A turquoise platter, with a layer of glass, on display in the garden.

OPPOSITE Reminiscent of a monastery, the bedroom is frugally furnished with an old family cupboard and bedstand, and cypress tree beams overhead.

At the edge of the eastern Peloponnese lie the islands of Hydra, Spetses, Poros and Aegina. From the 17th century onwards, successful Hydriot and Spetsian merchants and sea captains built magnificent mansions in picturesque little ports.

The tiny Hydra harbour is a natural amphitheatre and the tier-like, cubic houses were marvellously captured by the painter Ghika. In the 1950s Hydra acquired world fame due to the films shot there. This unexpected fame drew in jetsetters, who sought peace and inspiration living in palazzo-style mansions set against volcanic rocks.

From the late 19th century Spetses was regarded as a health resort, frequented by high-society Athenians. Austere, frugal and geometric, the architecture of Hydra and Spetses flourished when enterprising sea merchants dared to cross the Mediterranean, heedless of the dangers, hauling grain from the Black Sea to European harbours. They made huge fortunes by running the English blockades. Their enterprise and commerce inevitably influenced the architecture.

Elegant Venetian-style villas of two or three storeys, depending on the natural incline of the ground, built in L-shapes or open squares, carry signs of the Italian Renaissance, bringing together elements of East and West, the Aegean and the Peloponnese. With red-tile roofs, shady gardens, thick walls of chiselled stone, large and small arches, and balconies and terraces overlooking the sea, they often possess their own private chapel within the grounds. Their interiors sport monumental staircases leading to the formal room.

Some even boast a ballroom and a special Ottoman-style room for smoking water pipes. With painted floors and ceilings, stencilled borders round the walls and wood-carved ornaments, the rooms include not only remarkable furniture, but also paintings, grand pianos, crystal and china imported from Marseille, Venice and Odessa.

Alongside these grand abodes, small, simple, one-room houses with gardens follow the line of Cycladic architecture, differing only in their red-tile roofs. Motifs of birds, mythical beasts, anchors, dolphins and mermaids can be found in the pebblestone flooring of these humble homes and in the impressive mansions, narrow streets, churchyards and village squares alike.

Poros is a small, quiet island directly opposite the Peloponnesian peninsula of Trizina. The colourful, neo-classical houses are gaily reflected in the port's waters while the Lemonodasos' aromatic lemon copse submerges the island in its dizzying scent.

Aegina, known since antiquity as a great naval power, saw its days of glory in 1928 when it was the capital of the newly established Greek nation. In the idyllic landscape of pistachio trees and vineyards, rise the splendid villas with vast storage space for the harvest, while the wonderful Temple of Artemis Aphaia continues to attract visitors today. These islands, with the rugged beauty of barren rock, are above all the land of a daring people thirsting for adventure – liberators, heroes and heroines such as the legendary Bouboulina.

THE SARONIC ISLANDS

a house by the sea

A narrow channel is all that separates the pine-covered island of Spetses from the Peloponnese coast. Spetses lies so close to the Greek capital that for centuries it has been regarded as a health-inducing suburb for Athenians. Today, the imposing 18th- and 19th-century houses, built by wealthy sea captains and traders, belong to the Athenian elite or foreigners, like Isabella Tree, who have been captivated by the island's calm beauty.

English by birth and a writer by occupation, Isabella spent most of her childhood summers on the island. Her husband, Charlie Burrell, later bought her a villa there. The Spetses house became their favourite refuge and she often describes it in her travel articles published in international magazines. 'I was only too conscious of Spetses's charms...the cocktail of sunsets and retsina; the sensual overload of sounds and tastes and smells; the arching, impossibly blue canopy of sky; the glittering depths of the sea – all that was irresistible.' The house was originally built in 1860 by a merchant sea captain who had earned his fortune blockade running. The house was handed down to Mme Marchetti, his granddaughter, to whom the tiny island of Spetsopoula belonged before she sold it to shipping tycoon Stavros Niarchos. When she realized Isabella and Charlie were the perfect people to maintain the spirit of the place, she decided to part with it.

OPPOSITE, LEFT; AND OPPOSITE, RIGHT A window
surrounded by greenery; the courtyard is
laid with pebbles found on the beach next
to the house.
LEFT A view of the 18th-century Venetian-
style villa built by a wealthy Spetsian captain.
TOP The entrance, from the sea, to the house.
ABOVE Even the beach entrance is pebbled,
while the grounds are surrounded by thick,
whitewashed stone walls.

It took the young couple two years to expose the real beauty of a house that had accumulated a lifetime of bric-à-brac. 'It was like peeling back an onion', Isabella says. As they pared away the pictures, the heavy drapery, the carpets and the cumbersome furniture, they were able to get closer to the house's heart and let it come alive. Only the *saloni* with its large windows (now curtain-free) and all-encompassing view has its delicate frescoes more or less intact. In this magnificent room even the soaring ceilings, like the traditional floors, are painted a perfect powder blue, entertaining the eye before enticing it through the door towards the ageless vista

of the fishing boats bobbing in the sea below. An excellent local restorer seamlessly redid the traditional paintwork throughout the house when they decided to bury the electricity conduit pipes in the walls as 'they ran along the walls like spaghetti'. There were many areas where damp had destroyed the old paintwork so they had the tiles on the roof turned, damaged areas repaired and all the old, rotting windows replaced with new hardwood frames treated to withstand the seaside assault.

The staircase behind the arches with plaster mouldings leads to the upstairs bedrooms, which have a somewhat monastic air despite their comforts.

The house's charm lies in the welcome contrast between the original furnishings – wrought-iron beds, chests of drawers, china washbasins and pitchers – and the newly acquired pieces such as the comfortable white English sofas and wicker armchairs.

Life here is lived outdoors, much as it must have been when the house was built. Lounging or dining all day long on the vast patio terrace is a sheer delight with the scent of lemon blossoms and jasmine wafting over from the garden. Suspended over the sea, the terrace creates the sense of being on the most elegant of ocean liners ready to set sail on the open sea.

OPPOSITE The imposing hall has a wooden staircase leading to the upper floor and retains the original colours, the plaster mouldings on the walls and the ceiling, and the mosaic floor.

ABOVE, LEFT The sitting room, containing only large, comfortable English sofas, has a wooden white floor, high painted ceilings and walls with frescoes in the most perfect lavender.

LEFT A pair of French beds with painted wooden bedsteads furnish the bedroom.

ABOVE, RIGHT The upstairs hall is in the original colours, restored by a local expert who specializes in traditional painting. The ceiling lamp, like all the lamps, is also original.

a bouquet of history

'It took my breath away when I first saw it, floating under Venus like a majestic black whale in an amethyst evening sea, and it still takes my breath away when I shut my eyes now and remember it. Its beauty was rare even in the Aegean, because its hills were covered with pine trees', so wrote John Fowles about his beloved island of Spetses. Fowles's discovery of the island was profoundly significant for him, a spiritual experience that resulted in one of his most important books – *The Magus* (1977). No doubt Fowles was well acquainted with the two-storey house in the harbour since he frequently took long walks along the coast.

Built in 1840, the majestic mansion (known as a captain's house) is steeped in the history of the island. The celebrated family comes from a long line of sea captains who had their own fleets. They

have been recorded in Greek history as having significantly helped the island of Spetses in its first victorious naval battle against the Turks in the Greek War of Independence in 1821.

A fine example of the island's architecture, laid out in an X-shape and borrowing elements from Corsica and southern Italy, the large, one-block house on the sea, with its thick whitewashed stone walls and red-tile roof, is a perfect escape from the relentless summer heat. The spacious rooms are laid out symmetrically and the floors and the high ceilings are durable pine painted white. Echoing the colours of the landscape, the living room is decorated in shades of the sky and sea, though it takes on reddish overtones in the evening sunset.

The charm of the Greek, English and French furnishings is accentuated by the largely white

background, while the walls are adorned with paintings of ships. The whole house bears testimony to the owners' love of the sea, rendering the ship the theme of the décor: it appears in the paintings, on the porcelain tea services, on the pyrographed trousseau trunks and in the study with the model ships belonging to the owner's grandfather.

The owners left the house unchanged except for the ground floor which is paved with stone slabs from Malta and has been remodelled as a guestroom. It was originally used as a boathouse and as storage for fishing equipment, wine barrels, oil canisters and the water tank.

Over the wrought-iron balcony, the scent of pine wafts in through the windows, while the crickets play counterpoint to the waves below, languidly lapping against the *dapia*, the wall of the house. From the

OPPOSITE, LEFT The pebbled courtyard –
typical of Spetsian captains' houses
– is surrounded by a lush flower garden.
In the background the whitewashed, stone
stairway leads up to the house's main
entrance.

OPPOSITE, RIGHT Protected by the low stone
wall, *dapia*, that stretches down to the sea
below, the large terrace is ideal for lounging
in the wicker armchairs and gazing out at
the sea and the Peloponnesian coastline.

RIGHT The senses are awakened by the light
breeze and the lapping of the waves at the
wrought-iron balcony. This is where the
captain once stood to watch his fleet.

landing of the white stone exterior staircase you
can see the wild, lush garden, the pergola, the patio,
the wood stove and the many-levelled garden with
creeping ivy, hemmed in by a high wall.

The green and white pebblestone mosaic path,
with nautical motifs of mermaids and anchors,
carves through the lush garden of orange trees,
locust trees, begonias and hibiscus flowers, all
characteristic of the traditional Greek garden. Later
on in the day, when the sea turns a deep wine red,
one can lounge on the wide veranda and gaze out
at the open sea as far as the Peloponnese coastline,
while breathing in the heavenly scent of the lemon
tree blossoms, the wisteria and the jasmine.

LEFT Each piece in the large *sala* eloquently tells the tale of the family and the history of the land. Seascapes bedeck the walls. The hostess removed some of the pieces and painted the pine floors, the ceiling and the walls grey-white, bringing out the charm of the pieces even more.

BELOW The ship is the theme of the house and can be seen even in the old china set that survived from the owner's grandfather's ship.

ABOVE, LEFT On the mantelpiece of the
marble fireplace in the winter sitting
room sits a model of one of the family's
first steamboats.

ABOVE, RIGHT A carved wooden period
dressing table with a china water pitcher
in the hostess's bedroom.

ABOVE In the guestroom on the ground floor
the red in the cottonweave sheets interrupts
the dominance of white. The shutters on
the high windows are inside, a feature of
the local architecture.

east meets west

Nothing disturbs the serenity of mornings on the wide balcony overlooking the Old Port of Spetses. Nothing but the monotonous tapping on the pinewood hulls of the traditional caïques carried on the breeze from the boat yard where local craftsmen build the unique Spetsian boats worked by eye without plans, with the blueprint in their genes.

Like all the houses in the neighbourhood, this one was built by a wealthy seafaring merchant in the mid-19th century. Later in the 20th century it passed into the hands of Cyrus Schulzberger, an American journalist, and his Greek wife, Marina Landa. The house was in its heyday – it saw the likes of distinguished guests such as Greta Garbo and Elizabeth Taylor. In the early 1980s the house was bought by an Athenian family and architect Michalis Photiadis set about restoring it to its original form, removing any extensions or modifications that had been haphazardly carried out. He restored the sitting room

OPPOSITE, LEFT A guesthouse in the courtyard.

OPPOSITE, RIGHT Contrasting sharply with the rich interior décor, the architecture of the captain's house is austere and frugal. Built in 1855 by a seafaring merchant, it commands a spectacular view of the old harbour.

BELOW The entrance is flanked by columns; the motifs on the path are of the mythological figure Triton, a ship and the sun.

RIGHT This corner of the courtyard is the perfect spot for daydreaming and inhaling the scent of lemon blossom, while enjoying the view of the shipyards.

OVERLEAF, LEFT A bench from a Greek barber shop under the stairway leading to the sitting room.

OVERLEAF, RIGHT Classic Spetses-style grilled windows and Maltese flagstones can be found in the kitchen. The warm atmosphere is created by the Mexican tiles and a French refectory table with Greek *kafenion* chairs.

to its initial position on the first floor and installed a staircase connecting it to the kitchen on the ground floor. He also repaired the pebbled areas on the terraces and created new ones in the hanging garden.

The austere and frugal exterior sharply contrasts with the lavish interior where East meets West. White dominates the walls and wide-planked cedar floors, providing a perfect backdrop for the splashes of colour in the Greek fabrics on the island-style couches and the collection of images of fish, lending a modern freshness without betraying the spirit of the old residence. In the hall the high walls are muralled with the unexpected theme of the American Civil War, created by travelling Italian painters in the 19th century. The Athenian mistress of the house, having grown up in a family of collectors, wanted to give a naval note to the decoration of the living room with Greek and European furnishings like those the local sea captains would have chosen. Excellent authentic pieces are scattered throughout: the naval *cassona*, the Caucasian kilims, a tray engraved with a representation of 19th-century Istanbul. On the walls the figurehead from a ship

stands proudly next to the watchful eyes of sea captains gazing out. From the ceiling hangs a grand Baltic chandelier, which survived the rough seas, but received a thump from a children's football.

The lush garden has been replanted with jasmine and bougainvillaea, as well as with English roses and climbers. The side entrance to the house boasts a patio with columns and pebble-paved floors with Aegean naïve motifs: a mermaid, the sun and a ship. All lead to the marble springwell shaded by the lemon trees and the huge centenary fig tree.

The verandas and garden have been completely redesigned, with many levels, to provide a special haven for each hour of the day. Morning on the cool veranda, which has a pergola, offers a view of the white village houses tumbling down towards the port. At dusk everyone retires to the large veranda for an aperitif, while lazily watching the yachts and sailboats entering or exiting the port. And when the lights on the coast of the Peloponnese opposite start to flicker on the darkened horizon, there's nothing better than lying back and letting the exquisite scents of honeysuckle and nightflower waft over you.

OPPOSITE, LEFT The sitting room has furniture and *objets d'art* from the East and the West.

OPPOSITE, ABOVE, RIGHT A collection of Mediterranean fish on display in the kitchen.

OPPOSITE, BELOW, RIGHT An 18th-century, poker-worked naval *cassona* and hand-carved Italian wall lamp.

ABOVE, LEFT Typical Spetsian wrought-iron bed with a canopy.

ABOVE, RIGHT A bedroom furnished with 19th-century continental beds.

near eastern chiaroscuro

The beautiful port of Hydra, the quintessence of Grecian romanticism, delights anyone who sets foot on its quay. Ellen and Eberhard Baumann made excursions from their Athens home to Hydra eighteen years ago and fell in love with the island. Finally, they bought a house there and now spend their summers on the island.

Both German, the Baumanns met, rather glamorously, in Rome. They have lived a nomadic life with their two children in some of the most

exotic cities of the world such as Tokyo, Beirut, Athens, Istanbul, Cairo, Baghdad and Amman. They have completely different personalities, but complement each other perfectly. Ellen is an artist and possesses a great talent for decorating their homes, while Eberhard works for a large Swiss firm.

After much thought they decided to buy a ruin with a cistern next to their property. They found the owners, one of whom was living in London. They were given photographs that showed what the house

looked like in 1890. In order to restore it to its former beauty, the house was rebuilt with the original stones by a gifted builder, Panayotis Miras.

In the bright white port, towards which the houses tumble like sugar cubes, the captain's house made of local red stone has now been fully renovated and makes the proud statement that a hundred years ago few island houses were whitewashed. An unexpected Eastern world opens at the threshold of the courtyard with the terraced garden, hidden patios and fountains

of gurgling water. The building comprises an unusual combination of different architectural elements – some imported – inspired by the Baumanns' homes in the cities of the East, which results in a curious mix of eastern Mediterranean style.

The spacious living room area resembles their house in Amman; the bathroom is as large as the one in the Tokyo house and overlooks the courtyard, creating a ritual of sensuous pleasures; the fountain is reminiscent of their Cairo residence; and the built-in couches recall their home in Istanbul. Even the building materials arrived from different countries: the blue antique tiles from Iznik in Turkey; the ironwork on the windows was hammered into shape by a commissioned craftsman in Amman; the floor in the sitting room is a Byzantine mosaic crafted in marble, while the rest of the room is decorated in

OPPOSITE The natural terracotta pigments on the terrace harmoniously blend with the Hydriot landscape.
ABOVE In the sitting room a curious mix of eastern Mediterranean architecture reflects the Baumanns' cosmopolitan lifestyle, similar to that of the local 19th-century seafarers. The pink and green marble on the floor is from Jordan and the fountain from Cairo.
LEFT The intricate metalwork grills over the windows were made to order by a blacksmith in Amman, Jordan.
OVERLEAF, LEFT Handmade tiles from Iznik, Turkey, were laid on the kitchen counter.
OVERLEAF, MIDDLE In the shade of the bougainvillaea, a midday ouzo awaits.
OVERLEAF, RIGHT Ellen Baumann created the kitchen table based on a 14th-century design from Samarkand in Uzbekistan. She also painted the walls, the counter and the ceramic tile floor, all in natural pigments.

courtyard with an enchanting fountain. The house is heated by a modern system designed to diffuse warm air throughout the house. It arrived from Switzerland by boat and its 300 kilos were heaved up the narrow alley steps on donkeyback. Eberhard remembers when it was being installed and the local artisan told him, 'Nice design, but it won't function here. I'll fix it so it works.' And he did!

Furniture and decorative items from every corner of the globe reflect the sophistication of the couple's taste and their cosmopolitan lifestyle, which is not so different from that of the local sea captains of the 19th century, who brought home anything that took their fancy from Istanbul, Venice and Egypt.

Hydra fascinates the Baumanns because it lies on the cusp of two civilizations – Europe and Asia – that of their native land and that of the land they have come to love. This is why they chose it as their home. On this volcanic, rocky island, 'Everything is in extremes and full of life, from storms and torrential rains in the winter to balmy gorgeous days and calm seas to scorching heat in the summer, the sun burning the rocks', Eberhard says with a passion. 'There is a deep energy-giving power coming from those rocks.'

pink and green marble from the Jordan desert. Ellen designed the interior with imagination and care. Her skilful, artist's hands chiselled the plasterwork on the walls and the built-in furnishings, giving them a rounded shape and fluidity. She then used natural pigments on the walls, the columns, the ceramic kitchen tiles and the fireplace in the living room. The natural materials and earthy tones create a cosy, lived-in feeling. Because the interior of the house was designed by the Baumanns, it does not stick to local tradition, but rather serves the family's needs. There is an open-plan sitting room with a marble fountain in the middle, a kitchen on the ground floor and two bedrooms with marble bathrooms upstairs. On the lowest level there is an open siesta room with a hammam-style bath overlooking a secluded

Impressive forests, towering mountains, enchanting beaches, cities inhabited since the Neolithic Age, impenetrable fortresses reflected in blue waters and Cyclopean walls and palaces, Mycenaean royal tombs dating back to the 13th century BC, the Temple of Epicurean Apollo, the Epidaurus ancient theatre and ancient Corinth with its huge Doric columns are all part of the remarkable landscape of the Peloponnese, the southernmost part of mainland Greece.

Nine hundred and ninety-nine steps lead to Palamidi, the imposing fortress towering over the medieval town of Nafplio, the first capital of modern Greece.

From Nemea to Sparta vineyards and olive groves mingle with the columns of temples and the remains of arenas and amphitheatres. The glory of Mystras, the forgotten star of Byzantium, is covered with ruins of manor houses and is only remembered in the colourful frescoes of the churches.

The mountain range of Taygetos, reaching the sea-beaten Cape Tainaro – one of the entrances to Hades according to mythology – forms a barren and arid rocky peninsula in the wild and magnificent Mani. The small Limeni port was a hideaway for local pirates who ambushed Turkish and Venetian galleons. Dozens of fortress towers dot the barren mountainsides and steep sea cliffs. This rugged land shaped the unsubjugated population, organized in patriarchal armed clans, ready to defend their homeland. Only the 'Captain' (the leader of each village) had the right to build fortress towers around which the smaller stone houses, cisterns, oil presses, bakeries and churches were positioned, forming small family settlements. Wandering through the glaringly white villages and their quiet narrow streets, lined with simple tower fortress houses,

one is struck that the light in the Mani is perhaps the brightest in the whole of the Mediterranean. The capital of the province is Areopoli, taking its name from Ares, the god of War.

Monemvasia, a giant rock tossed into the sea, conceals a majestic Byzantine town and lies at the southeastern tip of the Peloponnese. Strategically located to control the East–West seaway, it is invisible from the land and remained impregnable throughout history. An imposing gate opens onto a tunnel that leads to the calm cobbled streets of Kastro, a medieval town. Six centuries ago, fifty thousand people from the merchant and seafaring community lived in this walled-in citadel built fifteen centuries ago.

Arkadia, Ilia and Achaia are western provinces scattered with villages isolated in the high mountains where the inhabitants still live according to customs dating back to ancient times. The interior of the simple stone houses is divided into two levels: downstairs is the domed storage space, while the living quarters are upstairs. This is where the signal was sounded for the beginning of the Greek Revolution against the Turks in 1821.

A visit to ancient Olympia is for many a dream come true. Just the thought that 3,000 years ago, in 776 BC, the first official Olympic Games took place here and were thereafter carried out every four years for more than a millennium is enough to send a shiver down anyone's spine. Sauntering through the site one can see the marble columns that mark where the Temple of Zeus stood from the 5th century BC and the *voulefterion*, where the Games committee met and the athletes vowed to uphold the rules. One can almost visualize the athletes proceeding to the stadium through the rows of huge statues of Zeus and hear the roar and applause of the crowd still resounding.

THE PELOPONNESE

an imposing structure

Monemvasia is undoubtedly one of the most impressive rocks in Greece, a huge, solitary mass in the sea off the eastern coast of the Southern Peloponnese. Moni emvasis means single entrance, which aptly describes this natural citadel.

A significant naval and mercantile hub in the east Mediterranean during the time of Byzantine rule in the 14th century, this perfectly preserved medieval settlement is strictly protected by the state as a historical monument whose structures may only be remodelled according to plans approved by the Archaeological Service.

Echoes of Monemvasia's prosperous and proud past can be heard with each step, from the imposing entrance gate, the narrow streets that conceal myriad surprises, the houses with the carved windows, the terraces built on vaults to the Byzantine churches and dark tunnelled passageways that suddenly open onto a blinding view of the sea.

The story of Haris and Alexandros Calliga is as romantic as the place itself. As a young couple, both architects, they found themselves in Monemvasia remodelling a friend's home. While they were wandering around the old town, observing the fascinating architectural features of fifteen centuries of history, an unusually high chimney stack piqued their curiosity. The ornate stack belonged to the town's biggest fireplace, housed in a building that was to become their home. Thus one project led to another and then another until what had begun as a temporary avocation became a life-long devotion to the preservation and restoration of the medieval town they love so much.

Perched on the inclined rock-hill, like all the houses in the town, this one, built on four levels, retains the architectural features of many eras and conquests. The front door opens into the sitting room which has a spectacular fireplace and a spacious veranda overlooking the sea.

A wooden staircase leads upstairs where there is an open-plan work space and a bedroom. The roof sports exposed beams and cane and, while the architects are working, they can glance through the windows at the sweeping view of the red-tile roofs and the blue sea beyond.

On a lower level, in front of the vertical rock, is a small den through which one can access a succession of rebuilt stone domed rooms. On yet a lower level is the kitchen, the dining area and the wine cellar. In a region famed for its fine wines,

the owners could not resist the temptation to produce their own.

When the house was renovated in the 1970s, local workers, taught the old-fashioned methods of stone and woodworking, brought materials on donkeys as no motor vehicles are allowed on the narrow cobbled roads. The renovation was something of an archaeological dig for the architects. Details indicating Byzantine, Venetian or Turkish presence were successively revealed. The limestone fireplace, for instance, dates back to the time of Ottoman Rule in the 17th century, but at the end of the 17th century alterations were made by the Venetians. In an environment with such strong architectural elements, the Calligas believe that it is important to allow the place to create its own impression, furnishing it sparsely with only a few decorative items.

PRECEDING PAGES, LEFT Through a vaulted passageway to the side of the house one can see a Monemvasiote street.
PRECEDING PAGES, MIDDLE The unique Venetian chimney stack is built so that whichever way the wind blows it does not smoke.
PRECEDING PAGES, RIGHT The terrace pergola provides shade at midday.
BELOW A wooden staircase joins the first and second storeys of the house. To the left is a typical Monemvasiote domed room.
OPPOSITE, ABOVE, LEFT An inclined ceiling of wooden beams and cane is the prevalent feature in the studio cum sitting room.
OPPOSITE, ABOVE, RIGHT The imposing 17th-century limestone fireplace in the sitting room dates back to the rule of the Ottomans.
OPPOSITE, BELOW, LEFT On the ground floor a modern-style kitchen overlooks the garden.
OPPOSITE, BELOW, RIGHT In the sitting room stone arches house a handmade chest, books and momentos.

a contemporary rural idyll

One summer Dimitris Varvatsoulis, at a time of soul searching, climbed the mountains of the northeastern Peloponnese to see Vlachorafti, a stone village in the heart of the Arkadia province, where his family had once lived – he saw the ancestral home that he had never laid eyes on until that moment.

Varvatsoulis was moved by the endless mountain ranges, the unspoiled environment, the *kafenion*, where the old men of the village pass the time playing backgammon, the warm welcome they gave him and the fact that they remembered his grandfather and his nickname.

Varvatsoulis's grandfather's house stood on the edge of the village, alone and neglected. The idea of bringing it back to life intrigued him. He wanted to create a getaway for himself and his friends, far from the fast-paced lifestyle of Athens. The large balcony, suspended between the earth and the sky, with its stupendous view, seemed to be the perfect place to rest and relax.

Built in the late 19th century, like all the houses in the region, the walls are made from the local stone. The grouting is exposed as the stone was not plastered over. There is a traditional wooden balcony, a red-tile roof and a *katogi* – a basement – where animals were once kept. The Athens-based architects Zeppos-Georgiades & Associates followed Varvatsoulis's request to respect the design of the house.

The architects created, on the foundations of the old house, a home that is a thoroughly

OPPOSITE, ABOVE, LEFT A beautiful blossoming apple tree in the garden.

OPPOSITE, ABOVE, RIGHT **Endless mountain peaks** in the Arkadia province and gurgling waters of the streams are the backdrop to the veranda.

OPPOSITE, BELOW Immersed in the fertile landscape, the hand-hewn chestnut balcony is based on the original design.

ABOVE The covered dining room is an extension of the veranda where family and friends gather in the summer months. The Greek refectory table and the inclined chestnutwood rafters steal the show.

RIGHT A rustically contemporary atmosphere is created by the handmade Shanon kitchen and the modern dining room set designed by the architects. The inclined rafters are of rough-hewn chestnut.

modern expression of a structure built with traditional materials and yet it services the needs of modern-day living. The open-plan living room cum kitchen is an extension, as is the semi-enclosed dining area that continues onto the veranda. The area below this huge veranda was remodelled into a comfortable guesthouse. Despite these additions, the house retains the character and atmosphere of the local residences.

The exposed chestnut roof beams, the window and door frames modelled on the originals, the floors laid with wide pinewood planks and the hand-crafted hardwood balcony were all essential so that restoration would result in a comfortable village home.

The bright natural light streams in through the numerous windows onto the off-white walls. The minimalist interior with only essential furnishings – some representative of well-known modern designers and some designed by the

architects – contribute to the airy atmosphere. It is only in the bathrooms that there is a variety of colour: terracotta, ochre, yellow and aquamarine are combined on rosewood surfaces, framing the marble sinks.

The stark interior is accentuated by the exterior: dark tones converse with softer ones, old materials with new. Under the long narrow roof sits the dining room, opening at the front onto the old brick veranda that seems to be suspended in the landscape. The stone staircase leads down to the garden.

At the back of the house, the garden is on different levels, designed by landscape architect Eleni Georgiades. She planted vegetables for the dinner table, cherry, quince and almond trees, but also left a large section with mountain shrubbery unchanged.

Spiritual peace and harmony with one's inner self are what this house is all about. Here the owner has discovered not only the great long-lost pleasure of solitude, the enjoyment of the mountain landscape, the sounds of the breeze rustling the leaves and the goat bells tinkling, but also the cheerful commotion of his children and their friends when they come from Athens for weekend excursions, rafting in the gushing waters of the Lousios River directly below.

OPPOSITE Simplicity and comfort in the large guestroom which is located in the new extension. The limestone fireplace and the wooden furniture were designed by the architects.

NEAR RIGHT Leading down to a sunken bath, the floor is made of cement mixed with terracotta pigment. The rosewood counter frames the Pendeli marble basins.

FAR RIGHT Yellow-tinted concrete was chosen for the guestroom shower cubicle.

BELOW The unexpectedly exposed rock pours into the bed fitted within a wooden frame in the open-plan guestroom.

LEFT The uniformity of the off-white tones soothes the sensibilities in the large sitting room with Nonna Maria overstuffed armchairs by Flexiform. The floor is wide-planked pitchpine and the window shutters close from within as in traditional houses. ABOVE Inspired by an Ottoman *ondas*, the large couch placed between the kitchen and the sitting room is perfect for lounging in front of the fire.

'Each day is a brilliant improvisation with full orchestra – the light on the sea, the foliage, the stabbing cypresses, the silver spindrift olives.' The charm of Corfu described by Lawrence Durrell in *The Greek Islands* (1978) was felt by many travellers through the ages who happened upon the island. It is said that Corfu may be Shakespeare's uninhabited island in *The Tempest*.

The serene sea, the maze of winding streets in the old city and the irresistible 'calm boredom' have attracted hordes of travellers over the years – Lord Guilford strolled about the Spianada Square dressed in a short mantle reciting Plato; the lonely Empress Sissy of Austria penned her poetry in the shade of cypress trees in Achilion Palace; and nature lover Theodoros Stephanides, who, as Henry Miller wrote, knew all there is to know about every 'plant, flower, tree, rock, mineral, animal, microbe, disease, star, planet or comet' explored the island. The island is the setting of the most romantic rendezvous in *The Odyssey*. The stranded Odysseus and the young maiden Nausicaa meet on the beach at Palaiokastritsa, where tourists flock today to seek Homeric thrills and where one can still enjoy a romantic boat ride in the clear waters of the caves.

Located in the northwesternmost part of Greece, Corfu is the crossroads between Western and Eastern Europe. The unique atmosphere of the island can be attributed to its history. Initially part of the Byzantine Empire, it was subsequently conquered by the Venetians, the French, the Russians and the English, while it never felt the yoke of the Ottoman Empire. Western culture marked and defined its cultural development, evident in the architecture – the old Byzantine fortress, the Venetian Walls, the Reading Society, the San Giacomo theatre (a faithful reproduction of La Scala in Milan), the street with Liston arches, recalling rue de Rivoli in Paris, and the Palace of St Michael and St George.

When the independent State of the Eptanisa (of which Corfu is a part) ceded to Greece in 1864, the island became the intellectual hub of the country, greatly contributing to the rebirth of the nation. With its enchanting blend of architectural styles, the main town brims with contrasting images that defy description. The centrally located Spianada Square or Esplanade – the second largest in Europe – with its delightful cafés shaded by towering verdant trees sports a large expanse of grass in the middle that often hosts cricket games, the Corfiots' favourite pastime. The surrounding hills and mountains are blanketed in silvery green olive groves and studded with quaint ochre and red-coloured villages. The village houses boast the distinctive *botzo*, a roofed veranda. Beautiful 18th- and 19th-century palazzo-style houses are scattered all over the island, successfully combining English and Venetian styles. The estates usually boast a large olive grove, farm buildings, stables, oil presses, bearing testimony to the feudal system of not so long ago.

THE IONIAN ISLANDS

the kontokalis tower

The view from the veranda of the house is breathtaking – ancient olive trees descend to the water's edge and in the distance you can see Corfu town with its old fortress and the islets scattered around.

It was the imposing entrance to the estate, the olive groves and the surrounding sea that, in 1990, first enchanted Alexandra and Jean-Pierre Mueller and led to their acquisition of this property in Corfu. Alexandra is a goldsmith by profession and was born on the island; her husband, Jean-Pierre, is a Swiss industrial designer and graduate of the Royal College of Art, London. They have travelled to many parts of the world, but ultimately chose this Ionian retreat where they spend six months of the year.

The tower was built in the early 16th century, during the period of Venetian rule, by the Corfiot noble Christophoros Kontokalis to whom the entire estate of the local district belonged. A wealthy land and ship owner, he fought the Turkish fleet in the Mediterranean and was knighted by the Venetians in recognition of his heroic conduct at the naval battle of Lepanto in 1571.

The tower, christened Iliò by the Muellers' daughter, is replete with history. Recently, a gardener digging in the grounds around the house discovered a coin bearing the words 'San Marc. Ven. Armata', which dated from around the 16th century. 'Outside, we decided to keep the tower as original as possible. We also preserved the old plants.'

BELOW, LEFT The Venetian portal, dating back to around 1500, rises majestically among the lush vegetation of Corfu.
BELOW, RIGHT A series of columns and stone slabs, unearthed when the renovation work commenced, comprise the entrance to the tower.
OPPOSITE, ABOVE, LEFT The Corfiot arch frames the estate's verdure that grows right up to the sea's edge.
OPPOSITE, ABOVE, RIGHT The veranda overlooks the town of Corfu and the islets.
OPPOSITE, BELOW The dilapidated tower belonging to a Corfiot knight has risen once more above the sea, with a contemporary outlook and appealing simplicity.

Inside, modern installations were designed to blend harmoniously with the old, thick stone walls. The owners believe that the remaining structures should be preserved as they were found and that the new reconstruction materials should form a distinct contrast. Two new floor slabs of reinforced concrete and their surfaces have been left untreated and uncoloured and similarly, the texture of the wooden planking on the ceilings is exposed. They used cement in its untreated colour and texture to expose its natural essence, together with iron, wood and stone.

The Muellers applied the same approach to the furniture and furnishings of the house. The Le Corbusier armchairs share their space with the coffee tables – made from stone slabs on castors by Jean-Pierre – which are in front of the fireplace and built with the same kind of local limestone.

The architect, Sasha, Alexandra and Jean-Pierre's daughter, wanted to create as much space as

possible within the narrow dimensions of the tower – its total floor area is only 160 square metres (1,700 sq ft). In order to achieve this she came up with a number of inventive solutions – the non-obstructing sliding windows and open spaces wherever possible. The interior staircase leads to the top floor where the master bedroom and semi-open bathroom are located and is reminiscent of an old sailing ship – a hatch opens directly into the bathroom space. Underneath the bed, the basic design of which was inspired by the traditional Greek island *sofa*, is drawer space for storage, while the mattress is a Japanese futon. There is a splendid view from the bed through olive trees over the deep blue Ionian sea to the purple Albanian mountains.

The ground-floor space, once a stable, was converted into a separate apartment for Sasha. In places the rocks of the landscape actually emerge inside the house, once again bringing nature into contact with the man-made environment.

Economy of space was also one of Jean-Pierre's major concerns. He designed all the woodwork in the house: the bed platform with its storage space, the staircase, the hatch and the cupboards which comprise a key feature of the house. The wood is chestnut, chosen for its resistance to the damp sea air.

The entire house, inside and out, has an air of tranquillity, of harmony. This is enhanced by the pure, simple lines, as well as by the fact that the whole family has worked on the place with loving care. Alexandra and Jean-Pierre say that, living here, they experience the great calm and intense pleasure of the natural surroundings of the island, 'In the winter, when the north wind is blowing outside, you have the impression that you're in a lighthouse, and in the distance you see the specks of light from the surrounding villages of which, long ago, Christophoros Kontokalis, was lord.'

OPPOSITE, LEFT In the sitting room the old stone wall has remained and mingles with the modern reinforced concrete of the ceiling. The floors as well as the table are stone slabs found in the ruins. The Le Corbusier armchairs add a finishing touch.

OPPOSITE, RIGHT In a hallway outside the kitchen sit a Swiss cupboard, dating from 1700, in which the crystal is stored and an English colonial chair.

BELOW, LEFT The bath is flush against the back of the bedroom cupboard and the trap door in the floor leads downstairs.

RIGHT Four stone slabs, a plank of chestnutwood and a Futon mattress make up the bed in the ground-floor bedroom. The mosquito net denotes the style; the cupboard adds a touch of colour.

BELOW, RIGHT The tower is long and narrow, and space is limited, so space-saving solutions had to be found. On the top floor, a large cupboard separates the bedroom from the bathroom. The Aegean *sofa* provides a sleeping area and storage space.

the villa on the hill

'The houses above the old port are built up elegantly into slim tiers with narrow alleys and colonnades running between them; red, yellow pink, umber – a jumble of pastel shades which the moonlight transforms into a dazzling white city built for a wedding cake. There are other curiosities; the remains of a Venetian aristocracy living in overgrown baronial mansions, buried deep in the country and surrounded by cypresses' – so wrote Lawrence Durrell in *Prospero's Cell* (1945), his enchanting book dedicated to Corfu. Set in this landscape, with its countless smells and sounds and colours, is the family house of Stefanos Vulgaris, just four miles away from Corfu town in the village of Gastouri. Since it was built, in 1715, the house has been the 'heart' of a large estate, which still yields a rich harvest in olive oil and wine.

As the visitor enters the estate through the heavy 18th-century gate he can feel the warmth and humidity of the lush vegetation within. The early morning light with its blue aura reveals the blooming magnolias, pink oleanders, rose bushes and petunias – dashes of vibrant colour against the rich green monotone of the English-style garden. A long path leads up to the elegant country house. This simple, austere, rectilinear domain was built according to the English colonial style with one storey: a few steps with a stone balustrade lead up to the imposing entrance – the belvedere. From here an unimpeded view stretches over the plane and the green hills dotted with villages.

Long ago, the ancestors of the Vulgaris family lived in Bulgaria, but when Constantinople fell to the Turks in 1453 they followed Thomas Paleologos, one of the surviving Byzantine lords, from the Peloponnese to Corfu. The Vulgaris were landowners and in 1524 they were given the relics of St Spyridon, patron saint of the island of Corfu, as a dowry. From 1530 onwards the Vulgaris were recorded in the 'Libro d'Oro', which implied high social status within the island's territories.

Over the years the family carefully furnished the house with grand English and French furniture, precious antiques, old Byzantine icons, rare porcelains, silverware and paintings. It was Stefanos Vulgaris (1881–1950), born several hundred years later, who left the stamp of his character most vividly on the house. A sophisticated and learned country gentleman, he studied painting at the Accademia di Belli Arti in Rome and later at Toledo

in Spain. His grandson and the present owner, Stefanos Vulgaris, cherishes the memories of his early years with his grandfather and recalls him vividly as he sips a glass of local red wine in the green salon under the watchful eye of a gallery of family portraits, some of which he has joyfully restored. Over a number of years he renovated the entire house, making no major alterations to the interior and restoring the walls to their original vivid colours. The furniture was also restored and even the stone slabs on the floors were realigned.

Outside, a maze of shaded paths converges on the coolest part of the estate, the wild garden, where cypress and laurel trees grow around an elegant French garden table. Here, in the middle of the garden one may hear the sound of the piano being played in the large living room.

Next to the covered veranda, *xechiti*, so characteristic of Corfu, young girls used to shell the almonds that were to be sold in the market. They set the walnuts aside in large baskets, so they could be stored and used by the household. A small door leads to a courtyard where the oil press, stables and store rooms have been converted into guest quarters.

Stefanos Vulgaris remembers the excitement he would feel, as a child, in anticipation of the great feast of the grape harvest in September, when the young girls from the village came to help with the preparation of the wine. His grandfather was a connoisseur and his wine received many prizes. The girls would sing songs at the well and, in performing their tasks, balanced the jugs of water on their heads.

OPPOSITE The furnishings in the sitting room – an icon of St Mark with a goblet from the Holy Table of a church, a Viennese piano dating from 1800 which is the same type as the one Mozart played and 14th-century silk tapestries – all reflect the grandeur of the house.
ABOVE, RIGHT With an air of past times, the kitchen has an old hearth and oven, and a buffet from Piemonte, Italy.
RIGHT The precious Venetian mirror adds a touch of glamour to the simple fireplace surrounded by English leather armchairs and family portraits.

aristocratic elegance

Standing proudly on a hillside in the middle of Corfu, with a breathtaking view of the southern part of the island and the Ionian Sea stretching to the coasts of Albania and the mainland, the Flambouriari residence is a living monument to the history of the island. Here, in the middle of the estate's vast olive grove, the serene old house is remarkably well protected from the bustle of island life, even in the height of the tourist season. Sitting in an armchair on the veranda, Stephanos Manesis reminisces about the ancestry of the house.

When the house belonged to Aneta Ioustiniani, who was descended from a Genoese family, it was hit three times by earthquakes and after the fourth time she decided to have it built on a rock. Sitting on a steep hillside, at an altitude of 125 metres (410 ft) above sea level, the 300-year-old manor house borrows its shape from the rock. The 38-metre (125-ft) long circular veranda appears to be an architectural miracle. Directly in front of it, with a monumental bell tower, is the family chapel of St Stephan. Legend has it that Italian architect Montecatini started its construction in 1703 and it took his sixty builders three years to complete.

OPPOSITE The grand balcony follows the line of the rock on which it was built. It was here in this Corfiot noble house that Empress Sissy of Austria took her afternoon tea, enjoying the magnificent view of the Ionian Sea.

FAR LEFT Through the dining room window one can catch a glimpse of the Corfiot bell tower belonging to the family chapel.

NEAR LEFT The Greek Orthodox private chapel of St Stephan with a fine Eptanisan-style panel of icons.

BELOW, LEFT Built three hundred years ago on a rock, the house appears through the oleanders outside the chapel door.

BELOW, RIGHT The Venetian-style, Corfiot red mansion with its colourful windows is surrounded by a vast tract of olive groves.

They followed the architectural models of the time, giving it great unity and charm.

The plain exterior of the house is strongly reminiscent of a Venetian residence – it was built during the period of Venetian Rule – but the interior is a distinctive example of a Corfiot manor house with two floors and an attic and a basement cellar. When entering via the original studded wooden double doors, one comes across the living room with doors leading to the games room, the study and the dining room. A strong trap door covers the staircase, which, in the face of danger, could be sealed off from the rest of the house; beyond it are six bedrooms.

The building materials come from various countries, for instance, the flagstones are from Malta and the wooden floors are from Uruguay. A few years ago Manesis's English wife decided she wanted to make her own decorative touches to the house. She kept the interior walls white, adding a few splashes of intense colour, such as the burgundy in the master bedroom, and also preserved the rustic characteristics of the walls and floors. She painted branches on the bathroom walls and hung romantic-style curtains and matching throws in all the rooms.

Towards the back of the house, the kitchen still has its original bread oven, beams and range, now adapted to a shiny iron and brass affair. The result

is a charming house in pastel tones with an English fireplace and classical, light furniture. A welcome contrast are rare pieces such as the Venetian bedroom furniture – as old as the house itself – which includes a dressing table decorated with pine cones. It co-exists with English sideboards, colonial armchairs, French *lit de repos* and some Corfiot furnishings. Its intrinsic elegance is also due to the distinctive red colour of Corfiot houses, unpainted for countless years.

All around the main house there are small auxiliary buildings – the oil press, the storage buildings, the servants' quarters and the stables. They are all connected to the main house via small

OPPOSITE The large sitting room has a striking charm with its stained glass entrance doors, soothing pastel tones and white wooden ceiling. The light furnishings with the Venetian mirror and the French *lit de repos* are typical of Corfiot farm estates.

RIGHT Old maps and a hand-painted china service in the dining room.

BELOW The symmetrical elegance of the sitting room fireplace surrounded by family portraits.

courtyards, while one of the most impressive features is the large fountain where the water flows from three Venetian mask-like forms and ends up in a trough from which the horses used to drink.

In Manesis's words, his home is 'a house full of memories'. It was given to his mother as a dowry from her grandfather, who owned one of the largest Indian export firms, the well-known Rally Brothers. Manesis's mother was seventeen years old when she arrived from India and could only speak English and Hindi, but she was able to adapt quickly to the Corfiot way of life. Inhabited by his mother's family for over 300 years, today Manesis owns 7,400 acres of land, which amounted to more than 74,000 in his mother's day when the estate included 2,650 olive trees and produced significant quantities of olive oil and wine.

Peace reigns over the imposing veranda where Empress Sissy of Austria would arrive by horse-drawn carriage from Achilleion, her villa, and sip her afternoon tea while she enjoyed the timeless view.

OPPOSITE One of the bedrooms with wrought-iron beds and a showcase of dark wood.
LEFT The original water heater is still operational in the old-fashioned bathroom with stencilled walls and flagstone flooring.
ABOVE A built-in bread oven and a *moskiera*, a cupboard for keeping foodstuffs, give an air of the traditional in the kitchen.

Epirus, the northwestern-most part of Greece, is known for its unique stone villages and variegated landscape of mountains, wild gorges, rivers, thick evergreen and chestnut forests, alpine lakes and beaches with crystal clear waters. The capital of the province, Ioannina, exudes an oriental air with minarets, mosques, an old flea market, silver workshops and traditional *kafeneia*.

To the north, the Zagorohoria, comprised of forty-five villages, scale Mount Pindos and are surrounded by rare species of flora and fauna; the rivers are adorned with elegant arched bridges and Byzantine monasteries cling to the steep cliffs. The villages have distinctive cubic stone houses and slate roofs, striking a singular and austere note in the lush greenery. Their heavy and solid forms provide little variety. There are only windows on the first floor, protecting against the rain, wind, bandits and Turkish invaders. In the 18th century the inhabitants were rich merchants who traded with Venice and central Europe. Today, many of these houses have been remodelled into quaint hotels.

To the east lies the village of Metsovo with its imposing houses sporting the distinctive *sachnisi* – the part of the second floor that protrudes on thick beams. Known for its stock-breeder inhabitants, who still speak a special dialect of Latin origin called *vlahika*, in contrast to the rest of Epirus, it bustles with life. To the south of Ioannina is Tzoumerka, whose villages are untouched by time. The locals keep up the age-old tradition of stone building. Even further south, the twenty-four villages of the Pelion peninsula, with their beautiful, tall manor houses overlooking the Aegean from a great height, are the work of Epirus artisans.

The inhabitants of Pelion built their glorious residences skilfully marrying European and Turkish influences, using imaginative solutions to combat the weather conditions and popular wisdom to create a sense of harmony. Initially in the 17th century they built sparse and austere fortress-style towers with windows only on the highest floors where the dwellers resided. Later in the 18th century the manor houses became more embellished, featuring a kind of bay window on the top floor that protrudes over the first floor and a series of stained-glass windows that regulated the ventilation. This part of the house had wooden carved ceilings with geometrical motifs, carved doors and painted niches – the family spent the summer there while they lived out the winter on the middle floor which had large wooden couch beds and a Turkish-style conical fireplace. At the end of the 19th century the houses became even grander due to the immigrants from Egypt who introduced European, Renaissance and Baroque style elements.

Travelling through the picturesque mountain villages today, the visitor can look out on both the calm Pagasitikos Bay with the fishing villages enveloped in olive groves and on the crystalline waters of the Aegean. This is a feature that no other part of Greece can boast and is why in the wintertime you can ski down the snowy mountain, while watching the caïques bobbing on the Aegean.

THE MAINLAND

the excitement of the austere

The sun rises late in Mikro Papigo, a mountain village in the region of Epirus, the rays blocked by huge boulders looming above the village. Tucked in the side of Mount Tirfi at an altitude of 3,600 ft (1,100 m), the village's adobe-style houses of grey stone seem to be a natural extension of the surroundings. The village belongs to the famed Zagorohoria – immersed in thick evergreen forests, carpeted with 1,750 species of herbs, it looks peacefully down on the valley, at the bottom of which gush the icy waters of the Voidomatis river, a haven for trekkers and nature lovers.

From the village's central square a narrow cobbled street – originally constructed for cattle and rugged stock breeders – leads to a stone house where an Athenian couple spend their weekends. They were captivated by the charm of the Papigo lifestyle – the scent of coal and wood-burning fires wafts from the chimneys of neighbouring houses.

Built in 1860 at the top of the village, the house is surrounded by high walls. The entrance is a wooden garden door, wide enough for the cattle that once returned after a day grazing in the mountain meadows. When the spring warmth allows, the house dwellers relax in the paved courtyard while gazing out at the mountain landscape.

A typical example of Epirus architecture, the austere exterior, interrupted only by the chimneys, is a solid, two-storey structure with a slate roof. Crossing the threshold of the main door, one enters the *hayiati*, a spacious room with a flagstone floor, skirted by low, built-in concrete benches. The room exudes the warmth of Epirus with its colourful hand-woven tapestries, the dozens of old tools and copper pots hanging on the walls, the untreated cedar branches on the ceiling as well as the aroma of herb pie coming from the kitchen upstairs.

PRECEDING PAGES, LEFT Below the gigantic,
imposing boulders of Astraka in the Epirus
village of Mikro Papigo, the stone farmhouse
blends in perfectly with the natural
environment.

PRECEDING PAGES, RIGHT From the veranda
the view stretches to the mountaintops of
Tirfi, part of the Vikos-Aoos National Park,
where a plethora of rare species of flora and
fauna thrive.

OPPOSITE, LEFT The mosaic path of stones leading to the pantry is a true work of art.

OPPOSITE, ABOVE, RIGHT A typical feature of Epirus architecture is the wide, wooden garden door; the roof of wood and slate protects from the heavy snowfalls.

OPPOSITE, BELOW, RIGHT The greenhouse allows the mistress of the house to grow vegetables all winter long. She later transplants them to the garden of the 750-acre estate.

ABOVE Herb pie and brawn, accompanied by vegetables, made using the farmstead's produce.

ABOVE, MIDDLE Tomato sauce, pickles, chutneys, marmalades and liqueurs are produced in the summer.

ABOVE, RIGHT Casks of the house wine are stored in the pantry.

RIGHT Here in the stables, once the home of the farm animals, all sorts of farm tools are kept. The old low chair and stools were handmade locally.

Climbing the wooden staircase, you happen upon the *krevata*, an open area for receiving guests which has doors all around leading to the bedrooms. Next to it is the kitchen, *mangato* in the local dialect, the warmest room in the house. The flames flicker in the hearth and are reflected in the copper pots and pans that do not play a decorative role, but are used in the daily preparation of meals. At the centre of the long, wooden monastery table a fruit tart, made with produce from the garden, awaits. The sitting room, known as *ondas*, the brightest room in the house, sports a series of windows, a wide-planked wooden ceiling and low couches (*basia*) that double as beds. In the middle, the open fireplace, typical of Epirus, is the heart of the home.

The owners did not wish to make major alterations to the house as it had already been restored by the previous owners who had respected the original form and run it as a small hostel. They merely had the wiring, plumbing and heating repaired and double glazing installed to insulate the house from the cold winters. Indeed, their wish had been to acquire a house that bore no resemblance to their Athens residence.

The furnishings are tasteful and imaginative – chosen from antique shops in the capital and include hand-painted chests, peasant-style wardrobes, commodes and a collection of small, wooden animal figurines. The couple also love to collect, from the surrounding region, farming and household objects that are becoming rare: wooden stamps for bread, distaffs, sock needles and a myriad of other such interesting knick-knacks.

In the northern part of the estate there is a greenhouse in constant use. Here time passes quickly with the planting of flowers and vegetables, which are then transplanted to the garden. The house guests pitch in with the chores and are rewarded with a glass (or two) of wine produced by the host – the gardening often ends up as a party with much singing and dancing. Daily walks on the mountain are also a source of supplies. Everyone enthusiastically gathers chestnuts, hazelnuts, dandelions, mushrooms, cranberries and blueberries that end up as liqueurs, marmalades, chutneys and pickles preserved in jars of vinegar set out to ferment in the sun. Two large stone stables are the perfect pantries for all these delicacies. Also stored there are large casks of wine, the local *tsipouro* – a strong spirit – while the large cupboards are filled with colourful vases which hold supplies for the long, cold winter months spent waiting for the 16-foot (5-metre) snow drifts blocking the doors to melt.

OPPOSITE **In a corner of the hall, some of the 'plunder' from a morning walk on the mountain: fruit, chestnuts and walnuts.**
ABOVE, LEFT **The kitchen ceiling – like all the upstairs rooms – is made of wooden planks. The door leads to the garden.**
ABOVE, RIGHT **A cosy atmosphere in the kitchen with the ever-burning fire in the hearth. The locally made copper pots are used daily in the preparation of food.**

OPPOSITE, LEFT A painted chest sits in the corner of the sitting room. The windows are shuttered from within and outside the iron grills provide protection from bandits and foes.

OPPOSITE, ABOVE, RIGHT The sitting room door, typical of the region, is framed in pinewood.

OPPOSITE, BELOW, RIGHT A collection of Russian wooden figurines.

ABOVE The Epirus-style fireplace is the dominant element of the sitting room or *ondas*. It has more windows than any other room and is the perfect retreat on cold winter days when weather does not permit venturing out for walks.

RIGHT Even the tiniest room like this bedroom sports a fireplace in Epirus.

the lure of the primitive

The landscape of the Pelion peninsula in central Greece is edged by a series of bays and inlets and caressed by the sirocco winds. The farmhouses of the region, concealed in the thick shade of the olive trees, look out onto the vast sea. In their courtyards cats bask in the sun and figs are laid out to dry.

A huge rock spur on the mountain points out towards the sea and on it, among the olive groves, sits a little stone hut where the olives were once gathered and pressed in autumn. It has been transformed by the Greek architect Katerina Tsigarida into a summer house for her and her family. She has discreetly created a complex of flagstone paths, covered terraces, verandas and tables which harmoniously complement the surroundings.

The new structure is rectangular in shape, with a big terrace on the short face which overlooks the sea beyond the cliff's edge. Primitive and elemental, like a shell protecting man, it draws its nature from the site itself and is made of the surrounding stone. It is so well adapted to the rock that it ties in perfectly with the landscape, it is as if it has always been there.

The main structure is a small, one-room house. A roofed walkway connects it to the kitchen so that when the kitchen's double door is open it becomes integrally connected to the main house. Further on, hidden among the olive trees, the old hut has been converted into a guesthouse. Weaving their way through the lentisk bushes, myrtle and olive trees, the steps follow the ground's natural incline and lead to the swimming pool. This stone-paved patio and the oblong-shaped pool, which seems like a natural hollow in the rock near the sea's surface, are the perfect place to find some privacy and sun bathe.

The philosophy behind the style of the house is back to basics – it is elementary and Spartan – and it contains objects that have always met people's basic needs: a built-in bed, a stone couch, a wooden monastery table. Everything in the house is functional. It is long and narrow because it follows the line of the rock; the openings are small to keep the house cool; there is a lack of colour to soothe the mind; the walls remain unplastered to keep the décor natural; and the built-in tables are positioned in such a way that they are kept in the shade at certain times of the day.

The natural materials – stone, wood and cement – stress the idea of primitiveness and unify the interior with the exterior. The floor is paved with greenish grey flagstones from the neighbouring quarry; the ceiling is supported by thick beams from old tobacco factories; the veranda is paved with natural-coloured cement, using immemorial crafts, which have been deployed with great care and skill.

Designed to facilitate carefree living in the country-side, every building has a separate function and the house satisfies modern man's need to rid himself of anything superfluous in order to feel free in the company of the air and the sea that are so vital to him.

It is no wonder that the hut received the 1999 International Architectural Review ar+d award for up and coming architects. Peter Davey, one of the organizers of the competition, said, 'We were all touched by the simple and noble quality of the spaces. We knew the hut was in Greece and felt that Odysseus could have come home to it.'

OPPOSITE, LEFT Like a protective shell, the one-room house was adapted to the wild Pelion landscape. A roofed path connects the kitchen to the main house.

OPPOSITE, RIGHT Stone-laid paths around the house follow the natural incline of the ground.

ABOVE The rock removed from the veranda was used to construct this simple rectangular house with doors made of old olive wood. Here the passing hours are counted by listening to the waves breaking on the rocks below.

RIGHT In front of the veranda the natural sculpture of a rock juts out from the sea.

ABOVE On scorching summer afternoons
the corner with the stone table, built in the
spirit of carefree country living, is a small
oasis of coolness.

RIGHT Reinforced with concrete and slabs of
local stone, the swimming pool perfectly
blends in with the natural environment of
the craggy Pelion coast and the vast Aegean
Sea stretching before it.

THE MAINLAND | **pelion** | the tsigarida house 197

BELOW The sleeping area is on a slightly raised platform.

OPPOSITE, ABOVE Primitive and spartan, the one-room house is sparsely furnished. The rough stone on the unplastered walls lends naturalness to the monochromatic space.

OPPOSITE, BELOW, LEFT Lack of decoration heightens the sense of freedom. The built-in couch with cotton mattresses is made of local slate, as is the floor.

OPPOSITE, BELOW, RIGHT A weathered marble sink in the kitchen caters to the basic needs of a holiday lifestyle.

a stone tower by the sea

Stone-laid footpaths criss-cross like the branches above them on the mountainside of Mount Pelion. Here gushing streams and mountain springs abound and thick forests of chestnut and beech trees grow right down to the edge of the rocky Aegean coastline. This is where the legendary Jason and the Argonauts set sail on the Argo to find the Golden Fleece. The quaint, quiet villages with tall stone towers and manor houses with the characteristic second floor jutting out over the first are unrivalled throughout Greece.

The village of Lambinou is picture-postcard pretty and is covered with a blanket of snow throughout the winter and here and there brown shows through the snow in sharp contrast, especially on the foot-paths. In the autumn a carpet of soft oak and chestnut leaves leads to the tower that once produced silk and is today the country home of a family from the city of Thessaloniki. The tower is a tall, solid structure with fortress-style architectural elements: bastions, a raised entrance and small, grilled windows on the ground floor to protect the family from foes. You have to duck to go through the front door which has a stone plaque with the date 1846 on it.

Inside, where the farm produce was once stored, there is a comfortable sitting room with a dining area and a stone fireplace used on cold winter nights. Also on this floor is a sunken kitchen. A broad, banister-less, wooden staircase leads upstairs to the middle floor, the winter quarters, dominated by a fireplace and small windows.

The next floor is bright and breezy and appropriately named *kalokerino*, the summer quarters – in times past the family would have spent the warm summer months here. This part of the house is architecturally unique. The thick, chestnut roof beams are exposed and there is a series of small niches in the walls and a row of arched windows. This is an open-plan space – the concept was invented by the locals long ago – where one can work, sleep or sit and socialize on the comfortable banquettes skirting the walls. This room was also the kingdom of the silkworm. The dwellers would spread mulberry leaves on the long wooden shelves and the silkworms nibbled away at them, hatching the cocoons in forty days. The women then collected them and spun them into silk thread.

When the current owners came across the house a few years ago they fell in love with it at once and did not want to make any changes, devoting all their efforts to renovating it in the best possible way. The interior stone walls were bonded together with white cement, mud and lime; the wide wooden planks of the floors and stairs were left unpainted; and where they wanted to add an interior wall they used a large wooden cupboard. The mistress of the house wanted to retain the style and customs of the place with bursts of colour in the rugs and upholstery, and chose local antique furniture and hand-painted chests. The courtyard was paved so that the family could enjoy it all year round. From here there is a panoramic view of the red-tile roofs of the village houses and the open expanse of the Aegean.

The thick stone walls ensure cool summers and warm winters. The family takes advantage of all the seasons, hiking through the snowy forests in the winter and bathing in the crystal clear sea in the summer. The house marries eastern influences with traditional Greek style and adapts to the climate, creating a cosy atmosphere.

OPPOSITE All the architectural features of the silkworm house were repaired or preserved.
ABOVE The 1846 house, with its protruding embrasure, stands proudly in Pelion with the sea behind it.
FAR LEFT The low entrance betrays the fortress style of the house and through it one has a view of the courtyard paved with flagstones.
NEAR LEFT Snow and sea on the veranda with a view of Lambinou village.

ABOVE All bedrooms in mainland Greece used to be heated by a simple stone fireplace like this one.

RIGHT The dining room and its new stone fireplace were created on the ground floor where the animals were once kept.

OPPOSITE, ABOVE, LEFT High, arched windows allow the sunlight to stream in, which aided the hatching of the silkworm in its cocoon.

OPPOSITE, BELOW, LEFT Perfect for curling up on a cold winter day, the sitting room is decorated with traditional hand-woven cushion covers.

OPPOSITE, RIGHT A hand-painted chest and chairs from Epirus furnish the sitting room that was once devoted to the production of silk. The beautiful stonework of the walls was repaired as was the embrasure in the background.

an ancestral home

Situated in the mountains of Pindos at a height of 1,150 metres (3,370 ft), Metsovo is an attractive, prosperous village in Epirus, with wild forests full of bears. Despite being on the tourist trail, it is a place that holds fast to tradition while teeming with vitality. In the narrow cobbled streets you can still see women proudly sporting their elaborate, traditional costumes and the interiors of their homes show off the skill of their weaving techniques.

Brimming with light, rich colours and memories, the ancestral home of the Averoffs, one of the most illustrious Greek families in the history of the land, is a true landmark. As merchants and politicians, the Averoff men amassed their great fortune through cotton trade in Alexandria, Egypt and endowed much of it to the erection of public buildings in both Athens and Alexandria. Today, the house is the permanent home of European MP Yiannis Averoff, mayor of the town for many years,

his wife Elena, the instigator of the revival of Metsovian cottage industries, and their three children, who visit them during the holidays.

Originally built in 1726, the house was damaged during the German Occupation in the Second World War. In 1957 the well-known Greek architect Constantinos Doxiadis renovated the place. He retained the original building, the rather austere, x-shaped stone structure with small windows on the ground floor (all covered with iron grills which once protected against bandits and invaders), the window and door frames, and the wood-carved ceilings. Local building materials were employed: stones from the surrounding mountains for the walls, firwood for wide-planked floors and white pinewood for the ceilings. A large covered door leads to the flagstone courtyard. Behind the heavy wooden front door there is a highly practical 'mud room', where muddy boots and skis can be left and also the living quarters with three bedrooms, a kitchen and a children's playroom, where the Averoffs' young twin grandchildren reign over the joyous chaos. Traditionally, the ground floor of a Metsovian

residence housed the cows and sheep, the first floor was for the members of the household and the top, just under the steeply sloping eaves, was for storing goat wool, used by the women for loom weaving all winter long.

The narrow wooden staircase, topped by a trap door, leads upstairs to the large open *sala* where guests were customarily received. This room, like all the rooms of the house, has an eastern air about it. Low wooden banquettes decorated with cushions in colourful, hand-woven, woollen covers create a cosy and inviting atmosphere awash with light. Wood dominates the décor, like the wooden shelf running all around the wall, which is also decorated with large portraits of important family members. The 1920s dining room set is complemented by a wall display of old pistols and swords dating back to the liberation of Epirus from the Turks in 1912.

Next to the *sala* is the *ondas*, the richly ornamented room where the whole family gathers on cold winter nights. The room radiates out from the central, circular fireplace, the hearth of the home. It is decorated with a woven covering,

whose motifs of plants, animals and the local river are symbolic. The wood-carved ceiling, with a centrepiece carved by a local craftsman, symbolizes the sky, in other words, the presence of God in the house.

The rest of the house sports large bedrooms with space for everyone, built-in wooden cupboards and many splashes of colour with hand-woven tapestries and curtains. The result is a stunning family home with windows commanding beautiful views over the village and mountains, and family heirlooms exuding a warm feeling of history.

OPPOSITE, LEFT Austere in style, the home of the Averoffs – a family of livestock breeders and merchants – rises in the centre of the village.
OPPOSITE, RIGHT The master bedroom, decorated with colourful Metsovian hand-woven fabrics, features wide-planked floors and ceilings.
ABOVE, LEFT The cheerful children's bedroom in the local style.
ABOVE, RIGHT Grandmother Elena painted Greek folk art motifs symbolizing good fortune in the children's bedroom.

OPPOSITE Family portraits and historical maps
of the region on the dining room wall.
ABOVE In the chimney flue in the *sala* a small
pane of glass symbolizes Hestia, the goddess
of the hearth, who kept the fire burning and
protected the family.

Ancient and Byzantine, neo-classical and modern, marble and concrete, chaotic and contradictory, Athens has always borne the knowledge that its Golden Age was two and half millennia ago. Yet as the host of the 2004 Olympics, it was never closer to catching up with its glorious past.

Athens was liberated from the Turks as recently as 1830 and became the capital of Greece in 1834. Romanced by the classics, 18-year-old Prince Othon was magicked from Munich by the great powers of the day to govern the new Hellenic Nation. Avenues, squares and monumental, neo-classical-style buildings appeared, while wealthy Greeks living abroad funded the construction of numerous public buildings designed by famous European architects.

From a village with 5,000 inhabitants in the mid-19th century, Athens grew into a city with five million inhabitants in the space of a mere hundred years. The greatest change took place in the 1950s and 1960s when the rural population moved to the city, leading to a lack of housing. The city then saw the development of the part-exchange system known as antiparochi, whereby plots of land were acquired from the owner in exchange for an agreed number of flats in the finished scheme. The system encouraged the standardization of blocks of flats and was largely responsible for the way Athens looks today. Distinguished architects influenced by Bauhaus and Le Corbusier were also turning to the past in search of a Greek spirit in architecture, contributing to a new and promising post-war architecture.

With a photogenic topography of hills, mountains, coastline and, of course with the Acropolis at its core, Athens is a new metropolis, a concentration of essentially autonomous towns that have merged over time. Apart from the stereotypically picturesque Plaka area, Athens has many more faces: the northern suburbs of Philothei, Psychiko and Kifissia, oases of green space where fin de siècle villas stand side by side with ultra modern houses; Kolonaki with its designer boutiques; Omonia Square overwhelmed by immigrants of every nationality; and Glyfada with popular open-air night clubs.

Over the last decade, Athenians have discovered the charm of rundown areas such as Psyrri, Gazi and Votanikos, where industrial buildings and small 20th-century factories have been converted into multi-purpose complexes with theatres, art galleries, night clubs, trendy restaurants and artists' lofts. The 2004 Olympics led to various developments including the building of a new airport, a metro and the pedestrian walkways around the Acropolis and the spectacular Santiago Calatrava stadium. In addition, many museums have been extended and the Acropolis Museum is hoping to house the Parthenon Marbles spirited away from the Acropolis by Lord Elgin in 1801. It all signals Athens' openness to new forms of expression. Yet, while the Olympic ideals of freedom, democracy and civilization still hold strong, the 21st century undoubtedly belongs to Athens, the eternal city of the past and today a great metropolis of the present, a land of spirit and boundless vitality.

ATHENS

communing with nature

The internationally renowned Greek sculptor Takis chose a sacred hill called Gerovouno on the outskirts of Athens as the spot for his home and workplace. Three buildings, on a rock in a breathtaking location, overlook the Acropolis and the sea. 'Rocks teem with energy. The ancients well knew they contain ores and crystals, which is why they built their cities on their peaks: this is where the magnetic fields of the earth are strongest. It's little wonder that the Acropolis is built on a rock', Takis says.

The house is on three levels and has its origins in ancient Greek, Egyptian and Incan philosophy. The results, however, are plainly contemporary – flat roofs, open spaces, high ceilings and circular white walls laden with works of art give the impression one is in an art gallery rather than a house.

While Takis spends his week days in Athens, he takes refuge in his home in Gerovouno every weekend. The white house in lush green grounds represents the three basic elements of his concept for living: a location with energy, proper orientation and freedom of movement in space with direct contact with nature. Two of the three buildings, embedded in the earth, follow the natural line of the rock because Takis did not want to disturb the magnetic fields. He believes magnetic fields tend to expand in a circular formation and this should not be tampered with. For the same reason there are no interior walls in the house.

Takis believes that proper orientation on the four points of the horizon lend harmony and euphoria, so the entrance and the façade, with its large windows, point to the south, while the northern wall has a few small windows. The eastern and western walls create balance. The house is a protective shell, 'for no one can be exposed to all four points of the horizon'.

The main house is circular so that when Takis jogs around the 40-metre (131-ft) perimeter 100 times he has run four kilometres. Paraded on the white façade of the house are his *Aeolian Signals*: his means of communicating with the world and the universe as a whole.

The complex has separate buildings for the atelier-studio with a library, the kitchen-dining room, the forge and the main living space. In this spacious, bright room, with its cathedral-like ceilings that soar to a height of seven metres (23 ft), Takis explores great works of art, such as his 'anti-gravity' wreaths of magnets and the *Tableau*, which are magnetized erotic sculptures. Takis's works are collected by museums throughout the world – the Centre Pompidou in Paris, the Solomon R. Guggenheim Museum and the Museum of Modern Art in New York.

The ground floor is laid with old Greek marble flagstones, while the first floor is dominated by wood. This is where the artist plays the piano and often hosts dance classes and performances. The layout reflects his belief that his home is a 'beehive' where any artist is welcome to come and create within its walls.

The lush greenery surrounding the house is pleasing to the eye and is the result of another aspect of Takis's talent: he has employed an irrigation system invented by the Incas. Around every tree there is a groove 40 cm (15 in.) deep and 30 cm (12 in.) wide that leads the rain water straight to the roots, allowing for the automatic watering of the tree and full absorption of the fertiliser on the surface.

As the sun sets and light gives way to darkness, his *Solar Cells*, which have absorbed the daylight's sunshine, illuminate the garden. Scattered throughout the grounds they lend an eerie atmosphere to the house, while the *Signals* gently sway with each soft breeze, seemingly communing with the universe and certainly communing with the appreciative onlooker.

ABOVE The white house surrounded by lush greenery represents three basic elements of Takis's concept for living: a location with energy, proper orientation and freedom of movement.
OPPOSITE Simplicity, comfort and light feature in the guest quarters on the first floor. According to Takis, the circular wall, the large windows and the high ceilings help the energy to circulate, while creating harmony and euphoria.

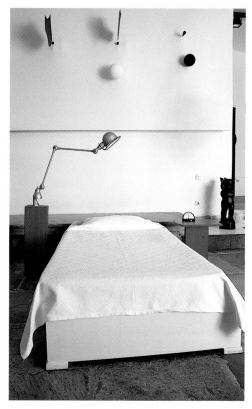

OPPOSITE, ABOVE, LEFT A table of weathered marble designed by Takis; and a sculpture.
OPPOSITE, ABOVE, MIDDLE White-grey marble for the roomy shower cubicle.
OPPOSITE, ABOVE, RIGHT The artist's plain bed is crowned by an 'anti-gravity' work on the wall.
OPPOSITE, BELOW, LEFT Takis's *Signals* communicate with the universe outside the workshop.
OPPOSITE, BELOW, MIDDLE There are no interior walls on the ground floor – only marble counters and sculptures such as the magnetic *Tableau*.
OPPOSITE, BELOW, RIGHT The bookcase follows the curved line of the wall.
RIGHT Takis's *Tableau* with erotic sculptures on the ground floor, which resembles a gallery.

suspended over water

Just a few miles from the city centre, Palio Psychiko is one of the most attractive Athenian suburbs, an oasis of green parks and villas with elegant gardens. This is where an Athenian couple decided to make their home with their four children, and their dogs and cats. Modern lines, spacious rooms that let in the light, large glass surfaces bringing the outside in, a vast collection of art and the dominant element of water are features of this modern dwelling. The house was designed by the ISV architectural firm (B. Ioannou, T. Sotiropoulos and A. Van Gilder), which has changed the architectural profile of Athens in the last fifteen years, putting its signature on the trendiest restaurants, shops and houses of the capital. This house was designed by Babis Ioannou – a lover of symmetry and large spaces who believes less is more.

OPPOSITE, LEFT A glass bridge reveals the presence of water in the house and links the sitting room with the kitchen and den. Three works by the renowned sculptress Chryssa are displayed on the wall.

OPPOSITE, RIGHT Working with a very small plot of land, the architect provided an innovative and modern solution: the swimming pool passes through the house and culminates at the side.

ABOVE Simple, geometric form and the white of the Cyclades in the atrium containing the pool.

RIGHT The main living area is dominated by transparent and glass walls facing the atrium and the pool. The suspended bridge with its airy balustrade links the bedrooms on the first floor. Furnishings are kept to a minimum – just modern Cassina sofas, an open fireplace and the *Heads* sculpted by Pandelis Handris.

Despite the limited grounds and lack of a view he managed to create a house brimming with light, water and greenery. Inspired by traditional Greek homes with a central courtyard and the presence of water, the house radiates around the atrium with the swimming pool. The white walls and the clean lines are reminiscent of Cycladic architecture.

The azure blue of the Aegean Sea is revealed as the visitor crosses the threshold and finds himself on a transparent bridge suspended over the pool that passes under the house and continues on the other side. With the pool as its core, the architect created a simple arrangement of four units joined by bridges. On the ground floor the sitting room and dining room are connected via a plexiglas bridge to the kitchen and den. On the next floor, the five bedrooms – two on one side and three on the other – are spanned by a suspended wooden bridge. The imaginative idea of joining the rooms this way reminds one of amusement park funhouses.

The sitting room, the heart of the home, is an open space built on various levels; the first floor overlooks this space allowing all the rooms in the house to take advantage of the natural light streaming in through the glass walls facing the atrium.

The high fireplace creates an intriguing contrast: the horizontal plane of water as opposed to the vertical plane of fire. The architect's aim was to create a natural continuum of the exterior and interior. The homogeneity of the materials of the floors and furniture, crafted out of the same type of wood, and the presence of water inside and out underscore the harmony of the minimalist environment.

The only accent of colour comes from the artwork that the mistress of the house collects with a passion. Representative works by famous, contemporary Greek artists make up a permanent exhibition that extends to even the bathrooms and the underground garage.

The furniture with its simple geometrical forms was all designed by the architect. The real work of art, however, is the lighting: series of hidden spotlights run the length of the walls in just the right places, while for the dining area the architect designed a unique light fixture made of glass and steel.

The beauty of the house is complemented by the swimming pool and the surrounding garden, landscaped by Karolos Hanikian with purely Greek vegetation: olive trees, lavender, rosemary, laurel, cypress trees, climbing bougainvillaeas and oleanders. On warm nights family and friends gather for dinner in the barbecue corner at the edge of the pool. The intoxicating scents of the garden, the lush greenery, the romantic lighting coupled with the starlit sky conjure up a magical atmosphere that after a few glasses of wine might even lead to another dip in the pool.

OPPOSITE Every room is in direct contact with the outside environment – here the living room looks out onto the garden. Between the bookcases designed by the architect is Angie Karatzas's *Dancer*.
RIGHT Maplewood dining room set; the floor and the lighting were designed by the architect. On the wall is a work by Vlassis Kaniaris.

at the foot of the acropolis

LEFT A romantic atmosphere in the conservatory on the third floor. The columns, the ceiling and the floor were added during the renovation.
OPPOSITE, ABOVE, LEFT A modern couch and a painting by Maria Sevastaki in the bright living room.
OPPOSITE, ABOVE, RIGHT The Athenian neo-classical-style hall has elegant doors that lead to the reception areas. The floor tiles are decorated with scenes from Greek mythology.
OPPOSITE, BELOW, LEFT The laundry room on the top floor became a conservatory with a spectacular view of the National Gardens and the Plaka district.
OPPOSITE, BELOW, RIGHT Yiorgos Zafeiriou's 1930s-style study sports stucco walls. Wooden doors separate it from the library.

Yiorgos Zafeiriou lives in Plaka, the oldest quarter of Athens, which overlooks the Acropolis and the columns of the Temple of Olympian Zeus. It is an unpretentious workaday area that manages to remain relatively protected from the chaos of modern-day Athens. Zafeiriou's building dates back to 1915 and is representative of bourgeois eclectic architecture just before the emergence of Art Deco. He is happy in his old-fashioned neo-classical home with its spacious rooms, conservatory and terrace with a limitless view of the sacred rock of the Acropolis. An architect and civil engineer by profession, Zafeiriou had always dreamed of renovating a stylish house and preserving the architectural features and the quality of life of the turn of the 20th century.

Classical style, inextricably linked to the arts and letters of 5th-century Athens returned to Greece at the end of the 19th century, after journeying to Europe, with the imported air of the bourgeoisie and French *savoir-vivre*. The ornate façade has classical-style plaster mouldings and a wrought-iron balcony which reflects the taste of the first owners, an upwardly mobile upper-class family.

The first floor of the house is dedicated to Zafeiriou's work, while he lives on the other three floors above. An imposing oak staircase with an ornamented balustrade leads to the first floor where the office, the library and the guestroom are located. The wonderful murals on the stairwell lead to a central corridor on either side of which are the large sitting room, two bedrooms that have been joined

into one and the dining room. The rest of the floor is devoted to the kitchen and auxiliary rooms.

The third floor is a surprise. In a semi-circular conservatory, backdropped by the balcony flooded with potted plants, is the den – the perfect place for daydreaming and reading. Next to it is a bedroom and the patio. A narrow staircase leads to the top floor where the old laundry room has been converted into a conservatory with a 180° view of the park on one side and the Plaka area on the other, from which the rock of the Acropolis sprouts. An even better vantage point is the roof garden on the terrace.

The decorative features of the interior lend character to the high-ceilinged, brightly lit rooms: the marble fireplaces, the plaster frames of garlands running the length of the walls, the painted doors

with small panes of glass, the neo-classical columns with a gold patina, the faux marble and faux bois murals that came to light during the restoration of the house, the floor tiles with scenes from Greek mythology all exude the atmosphere of old Athens. Here the architect wished to breathe life into the old residence while retaining its authentic style.

The restoration work was carried out with due attention by the restorers and skilled artisans. The plug sockets were concealed in the running boards so that the walls did not have to be dug up; dropped ceilings were added to the third and fourth storeys; the wooden floors were stripped and painted white. The strong chromatic palette was improvised, taking its cue from the traces of previous coats of paint found peeling beneath the oil paint topcoat.

Only the furnishings are minimalist in style, with just a few pieces, most modern and some classical, purchased at antique shops in the neighbourhood. The unusual collection of brass statues of athletes, the murano chandelier and an Egyptian chandelier are some of the fruits of Zafeiriou's exploration of Athenian and European markets.

With the light streaming through the tall French doors, the aesthetic of both past and present harmoniously co-exist, inspiring and complementing each other.

OPPOSITE The sparsely furnished living room shows off the original style of the house with beautiful mouldings and natural wood floors. Over the marble fireplace a Yiannis Tsarouhis sketch entitled *Young Man in Mourning* and a bronze statue of a Greek warrior.
ABOVE Manolis Pandelidakis's *Angel* dominates the simple bedroom where the walls are stuccoed in ochre.
FAR LEFT Faux bois murals were discovered during the restoration and the oak balustrade was restored to its original style.
NEAR LEFT In the bathroom an unpretentious 1920s style prevails.

to my mother Maria

acknowledgments

Firstly, I would like to thank all the owners of the houses who very kindly welcomed me into their homes and allowed me to take my photographs. Without their generous hospitality and cooperation this book would have never been possible.

Also, a warm thanks to my friends Michalis Melenos, Anastasia Papaioannou, Lea Raka, Maria Demetriades, Marouska Chatzigaki, Eleni Sanikou, Eleni Potaga, Maria Kladakis, Irini Paraskeva, Nikos Saxonis, Ioanna Kopsiaftis and Lia Papaefstratiou for the enthusiastic and inestimable help that each offered me in his or her own way. In addition, much appreciation goes to the architects Tassos Zeppos, Eleni Georgiades and Babis Ioannou.

I would also like to give a special thanks to Thalia Bisticas, my translator, for her dedication, cooperation and understanding of my work. Lastly, a big thank you to the team at Thames & Hudson for their marvellous cooperation during the making of this book.

The styling of the houses was done by the author, except for the Furler House in Symi, the Manesis House in Corfu and some of the styling of the Grazia House in Symi which was carried out by Vania Kokolodimitraki for a feature published in a Greek edition of *Marie Claire* magazine.

captions: introduction and openers

p. 1, from left to right: The Tsigarida house, Pelion, the Mainland; the Stimfaliades house, Patmos, the Dodecanese; the Captain's house, Spetses, the Saronic Islands; p. 3: the Tsiringaki house, Mykonos, the Cyclades; p. 6, from top to bottom and from left to right: the Grazia house, Symi, the Dodecanese; the Halkiadakis house, Crete; the Clow house, Rhodes, the Dodecanese; the Grazia house, Symi, the Dodecanese; p. 8, from left to right: the Captain's house, Spetses, the Saronic Islands; the Demetriades house, Paros, the Cyclades; p. 9, from left to right: Spetsian sitting room, the Saronic Islands; the Psychas house, Santorini, the Cyclades; p. 10: Oia on Santorini, the Cyclades; p. 58: Symi, the Dodecanese; p. 112: Exopoli, the Lefka Ori, Crete; p. 126: Spetses, the Saronic Islands; p. 150: Vathia in Mani, the Peloponnese; p. 164: Kondokali, Corfu; p. 182: Epirus, Vikos-Aoos National Park, the Mainland; p. 208: Panepistimiou Avenue, Athens.

Translated from the Greek by Thalia Bisticas

© 2004 Julia Klimi

First published in hardcover in the United States of America in 2004 by Thames & Hudson Inc., 500 Fifth Avenue, New York, New York 10110

thamesandhudsonusa.com

Library of Congress Catalog Card Number 2003116899
ISBN 0-500-51165-9

Printed and bound in Singapore by C. S. Graphics

DATE DUE